A WALK THROUGH TEARS

A WALK THROUGH TEARS

Dot Roberts

with a Forward and an Introduction
by a Healed Dr. Ricky Roberts

Unless otherwise noted, all biblical quotations come from the King James Version.

We acknowledge all those who have helped us in this endeavor and all those who have given testimony to this miracle. We especially thank University Christian School for their permission to use the photographs illustrating Dr. Ricky Roberts was in "Special Education Class" and that he was mentally disabled at one time. We thank also those who helped in the proofreading of this manuscript.
We further acknowledge that New Covenant Ministries of Jacksonville paid for the printing of the first thousand copies of this book.

2nd Printing

Library of Congress Control Number: 2001130026

ISBN: 0-8187-0347-4

To all those who are without hope and dare to seek after the God of the Miraculous.

TABLE OF CONTENTS

Forward
By a Healed Dr. Ricky Roberts

In this book are the lives, the sufferings, and the progress of many years of struggling against the onslaught of Satan for the sole purpose of battling for me to be healed from retardation. Found in the pages of this book are tears and the fountains of cries to Almighty God.

The purpose then, of this book, is not for my mother to recount to you the complete history of my life as a retarded person. Being a Ph.D. I could have easily written a book like that myself and in a higher level of comprehension. But for what purpose would that have been? I saw, from the very beginning, that the true purpose of this book must be to focus on the miraculous background leading to the miracle itself, the cost of gaining such an amazing miracle from God, and the miracle's aftermath. Further, I saw that this book must be written by the one who cried bitterly for my healing more than all others—my mother. I am honoring her faith, her life, and her struggle for my healing. If she had not stood in the gap for me, I may never have been healed. Indeed, I may have succumb to the devices of Satan.

Looking at a person outwardly, we cannot realize the struggle and the hurt in which he or she has inwardly endured. There are many marks of warfare, even more than I can imagine, found upon the life of my mother.

Instead of praising her fight for her retarded son, many people (not understanding the life of a retarded child or the cost involved in taking care of him) seem even now to cut her off or become jealous of her endeavors. They do not know that what God was doing through her, He can do through all willing vessels. However, there is always a cost. Thank God my mother did not let the emotions, thoughts, and ideas of others stop her from pushing forward to touch the hem of His garment and pay the cost of touching the garment of Christ for a retarded child to be healed and raised from retardation to above normality. What is the cost? Intercession, putting God first above everything else, and giving God everything.

Furthermore, I am writing this Forward as the result of my mother touching the heart of Almighty God. Therefore, I am writing this Forward as a person completely healed from retardation and as a thankful servant of the Most High God. I can say nothing about my healing in any sense, except that it was an awesome act of grace. I am speechless and defenseless before the grace of God in my life. Out of the approximately fifty students in University Christian's "Special Education Class" over the years, only one did God's grace fall upon in such a manner as to heal him of retardation. That one was me, and my healing is for the glory of God alone!

As a completely healed person from retardation, I cry bitter tears over all those children and adults who have not been set free from retardation. I seek God for their deliverance! I seek that someone, even may be myself, will touch the hem of the garment for them!

The very awesome act of grace saved me from such a state of hopelessness that it can hardly be described. However, I will try to describe in very few words the state of retardation in which I suffered.

From the very beginning of my life as a retarded person, I never wished upon anyone the curse of retardation. I never desired or hoped the laughter, the jokes, the funny looks, the dislike, the detestableness, and the embarrassment upon my worse enemy that I suffered due to retardation. Neither will I ever wish the wrath of God upon the doubter of such a miracle.

The Ancient Civilizations considered retardation (like seizures) a curse from the gods. The only word that can describe "retardation" in all its disguises is the word curse. It cannot be seen as a blessing. Those who say that this is a blessing have never lived it. Those who say such things need to experience, just for a moment, all the effects of such an affliction, and they would never cry out with such senseless words. They are senseless words spoken in ignorance. How can a life of retardation be a blessing? I do not know! I do know that I would never want that "blessing" back! The power of God has healed me from that affliction, and I never want it back. I have been set free from it for twenty-three years. I do not miss a day of such an affliction but live in the deliverance from it by a mighty and merciful God.

Retardation does not kill physically but mentally. It destroys all elements of time, space, and dignity within a person's life. It can destroy all hope, all promise, and all life if God does not move and prevent it.

As pertaining to responsibility, there is no recollection of such a thing within a retarded person's life. For this state of retardation leaves in its path nothing but emptiness of mind and, sometimes, even body. The retarded are left the most miserable creatures of all creation. Apart from God, there is no glimmer of hope and no glimmer of promise.

It is this miserable state that has left many to believe the retarded are nothing but eaters, void of the privilege of being human. It was this philosophy that pushed for the killing of the retarded in Nazi Germany, and it is this philosophy that helps promote the murdering of the unborn.

With the morals of the present society, perhaps I would have been aborted to rescue society from an unwanted burden. It is their burden and the burden of the whole world! Why? It is the result of the world's sin. The more sin, the more retardation appears to affect humanity.

Think about it! If I had been aborted, I would have never suffered the horror of retardation. Yes! But God would have been robbed of a miracle. Retardation is not God's fault but our own! I do not accuse God for me having been retarded. I point back to the sin of man as its root cause.

In my life I lived in my own little retarded world. I did not worry about how my life would be as a man in my early years. The retardation blinded me from all the hopelessness I would face as an adult if God did not move and bring a miracle upon my life.

If it were possible for embarrassment to kill, it would have murdered me countless times. My whole life, as a retarded child, was filled with embarrassment. Embarrassment in learning, living, walking, eating, weight, talking, inability to read, inability to have friends, and inability to express myself as God intended. In essence, the first sixteen years of my life can best be described as a Greek Tragedy with disappointment and tragedy after disappointment and tragedy. When there was some type of hope that I could live a partially normal life in this world, disappointment and tragedy would raise their ugly head and destroy it. No peace was there!

Such was my retarded life that I had to pay to have friends. Such was this life that I always felt alone even in the midst of a crowd. I always felt that I was an outcast, and I was never able to fit in anywhere. I always felt as though I was on a dunghill thrown there by Satan and the world. I always felt as though I was in a field of rejects that Satan and the world had thrown away. I even felt like I was a broken vessel, which was thrown away. In essence, I saw myself as the worst of the worst and the most miserable of the most miserable. All the time of my retardation, no happiness was found. In essence, I had no life. I lived, yet, there was no life in my emotions, my thoughts, and my mind. Mentally, I was as the walking dead or a zombie. Though my mind was corrupted by the state of retardation, my spirit was normal and cried out for healing from God under the power of the Holy Spirit.

I can recall the many times in which I found myself pretending to read and yet could not read a word. It was very common for me to enter the barber shop and pretend to read a magazine. The only things my mind could comprehend were the pictures. Picking up a book was horrible; I saw a book as a horrible barrier and as such a monster that I could not slay myself. In the midst of my retardation, I became fearful of books, save the Bible. I saw books as my waterloo in which I saw total defeat. God, through His grace, changed my waterloo into my victory by healing a retarded teenager.

Since God has embedded in me the memories of my retardation, I can easily recall the times in which I was called "retarded," "stupid," "idiot," and "moron." I experienced untold harm and hurt from these words being spoken. It is wrong to say that words such as these never hurt. They do very terribly. My mind was corrupted but not my spirit. It was my spirit that knew the meaning of all these words. It was my spirit that sought after the God of the miraculous and cried out to God for assistance. It was my spirit that said, "Forgive them, they know not what they do!" Plainly, the harm and hurt from these words were because of ignorance and an abhorrence of an outcast. Why? A retarded person is not able to conform to normality and is seen as an outcast. People detest anything that does not conform to normality.

Even now I must admit that some people of the church look at me as an outcast or something strange. Why? These people cannot grasp the scope of the miraculous that touched my life. They cannot understand or do not want to understand that God reached down and touched the untouchable by healing him. They are satisfied with living their lives not knowing the extent to which God can come into their lives. He will fully enter their lives if they reach up to Him.

In addition, I must admit that criticism against me is common. For example, my education is criticized. It is denounced as useless. And even, when I was working on my education, a man prophesied that it was not God's will for me to study the ancient languages and continue in my studies at college. Neither was it God's will, as this man said, for me to earn all the degrees that God gave me the ability to achieve. Thank God I know His voice, and I know His written Word! That man's prophecy did not agree with God's written Word! How could I be able to go to college, study these languages, and receive these degrees? Not on my own ability and capacity! No! All of these things came from the grace of God shining upon my life as a miracle.

Remember that these people of the church are criticizing a man who was retarded and who was unable to read and understand. However, he was able to achieve all these things by the grace of God, which healed him. If the reason for their criticizing is not ignorance, then it can only be jealousy. Isn't it a shame that other saints would become jealous and even despise God touching a retarded teenager? I wonder if these people would still want me back as a retarded teenager. Whatever the cost for my miracle, I accept and continue to accept it! I will not grant Satan or anyone else their desire of placing me back as a retarded teenager! I will remain healed!

Those who have attacked my education I leave in the hand of God. God has said directly to me, "Those who attack the education in which I gave you, I will handle!

They are touching that which touches My heart! They are denouncing not your education but the education in which I gave you!" Further, God Himself spoke and said again directly to me, "Those who denounce and criticize such an awesome touch of grace upon your life, I will judge!" I beg that those who do such things run to the altar of repentance less that which God has said comes in fury against them!

In the first edition of this work, I was highly criticized about how this work was written. The critics ask, "How could I allow the work to be written with errors?" The only answer is that God gave us three months to have the first edition out, and both my mother and I were struck by Satan in every direction during the process. The need for such a work as this is beyond imagination. Now, I understand the reason for God pushing us so hard for the first printing. People have been healed, set free, saved, and other acts of God have taken place simply by reading this work. In this world, God works through imperfect vessels. In the first edition, it is always common to have errors.

A prophetess prophesied, "Only those who do not know the heart of Christ would find fault about this testimony and this book; only those who are not seeking after the God of the miraculous would denounce it; only those who are senseless to My touch in My child's life would reject such as this." I beg God for mercy upon them all!

As the reader will discover, the aftermath of such an awesome act of grace continues. I have been led in many ways as God so directed. I was directed to go to college; I was directed to study ancient languages and theology; I was directed to form a ministry. All of this came from one who could not comprehend or understand any of these things by his own ability. I could do or gain nothing myself. But God shined forth His grace in the form of a healing and a miracle upon my life as a means of showing that He will take the useless and use it.

In March 1999, I founded a nondenominational ministry known as "True Light Ministries," based upon 1 John 2:8. Its purpose is defined as, "We follow the 'Old Way' already trodden down by the early church in its first three hundred years and follow their landmarks back to the cross and back to the Original Christian faith. This Christian Organization sets out to study the Word of God in the original languages and to prove what is being taught was, in fact, what the early church taught."

Since the founding of the ministry, there have been more than two thousand confirmed healings, miracles, and deliverances and more than two hundred fulfilled prophecies in less than two years. Further, there have been several manifestations of golden flakes fulfilling Psalms 68:13 and countless manifestations of flowing oil upon walls, windows, and the foreheads of people fulfilling Zechariah 4:14 and the belief in the fresh oil, which is fresh anointing.

There was one manifestation of the oil that I will never forget. I had forgotten my bottle of oil. A woman let me borrow her bottle of oil. The bottle had very little oil within it. I said, "God will provide." As I was teaching the Word of God, oil multiplied within the bottle, and it changed from its normal color to a cloudy white. Everyone beheld this sign and wonder! I said, "Get your mind back on Christ and not on this miraculous manifestation." When I had ended my teaching, I lifted up the bottle and took off the top. When I took off the top, the most wonderful odor filled the place. Under the direction of the Lord, I tasted the oil. The oil tasted like a very expensive perfume.

This manifestation took place in Alma, Georgia, when I was thirty-seven years old and in year 2000. I was teaching on the Last days. The oil was to be used to anoint people when praying for them. This is in accordance with James 5:13-18 and Mark 6:13.

I firmly believe that someone else was called and chosen to have this ministry and the manifestations of the Spirit within it. I firmly believe that person rejected his or her calling and election, and God (in disgust and anger and for the sake of grace) began to look for one who would obey Him and do as He directed. God looked upon a retarded teenager and saw a hopeless life. He saw a broken vessel that the world would never accept. God chose the foolish things to confound the wise and the world (1 Corinthians 1:27). He chose me, the broken vessel, who had nothing to lose and everything to gain. I owe God everything. I owe Him my ability, capacity, understanding, comprehension, the mind in which He bestowed upon me, the ministry, the manifestations of the Spirit, and my health. I deserved none of these things. I still do not.

Soon after I was healed, the Lord Himself told me two very important things that have been burned into my conscious, "Ricky, if you forget everything that I ever told you, forget not that the One who giveth can taketh away," and "Ricky, I will never, as long as you live, take away from you the memories of your retardation. They will remain in your mind as a memorial unto where I have brought you from."

I praise God that He healed a retarded teenager for His glory, His grace, and the coming Great Awakening!

VERBUM IPSE DEUS

Introduction
By a Healed Dr. Ricky Roberts

Many years ago, even long before the dawn of the Reformation, a holy saint of God made a powerful statement. His name was Tertullian, and he was a leader of the church in the third century. His statement rocks the very foundation of modern theologies and all the theologies so fathomed from the Reformation. Tertullian, dealing with the apostate Marcion who defected from the early church, said:

> Consequently, it will be clearly seen of what the apostle speaks, even of those things that were to happen in the church of his God; as long He endures, so long also does His Spirit work, and so long are His promises repeated.

What force there is in Tertullian's argument! To Tertullian, those who deny the continuation of the supernatural gifts so deny the continuation of God enduring and the Holy Spirit still working.

The history of the church is filled with the manifestations of the Holy Spirit. Remove those manifestations, and not only is church history incomplete, but it becomes lifeless. History proves that these manifestations were not and are not of the counterfeit variety either, as some people may imagine. For these manifestations experienced by people were truly of God. Then, Christianity without these supernatural manifestations of the Holy Spirit is nothing more than a dead religion and a dead hope. Without miracles, Christianity is absolutely nothing. All that distinguishes it from simple theism are the miraculous.

The early church and the Revivalists, like John Wesley, all dogmatically taught that the supernatural gifts of the

Holy Spirit, with all their outward manifestations, had not yet ceased. When Reverend Middleton declared that the gifts and their manifestations had been withdrawn, Wesley cried out, "O Sir, mention this no more. I entreat you, never name their silence again. They speak loud enough to shame you as long as you live."

In the Great Awakening headed by Jonathan Edwards, there were many manifestations of the Holy Spirit. Some voiced such concern against these supernatural gifts and their manifestations that they accused the entire Great Awakening Movement of being in league with Satan. Jonathan Edwards refuted those accusations and preached on the genuine and counterfeit signs, affirming that what occurred in the Great Awakening was genuine. Indeed, Jonathan Edwards concluded that God can still perform miracles, speak to His people, show dreams and visions, and work all sorts of other manifestations.

In his writings Edwards describes many persons who, in his day, were the subjects of the high and extraordinary work of the Holy Spirit. He describes one person who continued for five or six hours in a vision of Christ. When the vision ended, the person thought that only a minute had passed. Extraordinary views of divine things, prophecy, tongues, and the like manifested themselves frequently in this revival. Some people for a time could neither stand nor speak; some had their hands clinched and their flesh cold but their senses remaining; others uncontrollably shook and fell to the ground. An extraordinary sense of the awful majesty, greatness and holiness of God overwhelmed the soul and body of all that witnessed these manifestations of the Spirit, and a sense of repentance filled the whole revival.

On the continuation of the supernatural gifts of the Holy Spirit and their manifestations Edwards confesses, "The whole tenor of the Gospel proves it; all the notion of religion that the scripture gives us confirms it." In his work entitled, *Mark of a Work of the True Spirit,* he says that the Holy Spirit "has brought to pass new things, strange works, and has wrought enough to surprise both men and angels. As God has done thus in times past, so we have no reason to think but that he will do so still." So Lord, do it again!

Did not Paul himself say that through mighty signs and wonders and by the power of the Spirit of God was the Gospel of Christ fulfilled in his ministry (Romans 5:19)? So, without the manifestations of the Holy Spirit, the Gospel cannot be fulfilled. No wonder the early church said that the Gospel of the Apostles was truly full or that the Apostles and their disciples taught the "full Gospel." The failure of the church at large today can be placed at none other than its rejection of the Holy Spirit, His gifts, and the manifestations of the gifts in the church. The church has demanded that the Holy Spirit have no place within His own church.

As one will truly see, this book is about the miraculous of God still being alive and well. It is about what God can do in the miraculous when faith is not blinded, is complete, and is not weakened. It is also about what God can do when a person looks not into the realm of the possible but into the realm of the impossible for assistance. It is about believing, along with the early church, those saints before the Reformation, and the great Revivalists, that as long as God endures so will His Spirit work. It is about proclaiming to a child that God is still a God of the miraculous and telling him or her to reach out to that God of the miraculous. It is a witness that in the craziness of this world God still performs miracles and healings. It is a proclamation to all the saints to retain their faith, no matter what happens. It is an exhortation to stand strong, no matter the hellish opposition that Satan may put one through. It is a vindication that along with the angels, *Our God liveth*! Too often the saint is told that Satan is alive and well upon this earth but is denied that the Lord God is too.

Miracles and healings of all sorts are the bread of the saints (Matthew 15:26). They are indications that God is alive and well upon this planet and that the Word of God has been and is so continuing to be sustained, substantiated, and proven. These manifestations of the Spirit bring liberty since the Lord is there and working before the people (Isaiah 61:1). Did not Paul himself say, "Where the Spirit of the Lord is, there is liberty?" (2 Corinthians. 3:17). How does the Holy Spirit bring liberty? Through His supernatural manifestations, whatever they may be.

The belief that God is still the God of the miraculous is the only hope you can hold onto when the storms of life are raging, and when the times of suffering so penetrate the lives of the saints that no hope is seen. This belief is often sparked simply by God promising (whether from the Scriptures themselves or through a word given) that He will move and perform the miraculous in a life. That belief becomes a pillar and a foundation upon which all the storms of life can roar against. Yet, there you stand like Daniel still looking to the God of the miraculous with an assurance beyond this realm that God will move and rescue you. Sadly, time is a killer of this belief, hope, and promise. Therefore, continue to hold on, despite the time you have spent. And continue to meet God's conditions, keep God's conditions, and fulfill God's conditions, no matter what happens. For as sure as anything, as the storms are raging in your lives, Satan will try his best to make you denounce the promise and cause you to lose everything. Because of this, it is very possible for a word to be given from God and never be fulfilled.

The storms of sufferings so raged in our lives that no peace and no rest penetrated our lives. Many times my mother would cry out to God for death as she was driving to work. The storms began before I was born and continued long after, even over thirty years. Only now do we see peace and rest coming upon our lives. Paul said to reign with Christ a saint must suffer (2 Timothy 2:12). My family and I are living witnesses of this statement. Satan often tried to destroy the lives of my father, my mother, and me. He sought to prevent the purpose and intention of God and may have succeeded if my father and my mother had not held on for life believing God beyond anything else.

It is well to remember that the state of suffering was seen by Paul to be connected to the highest state of grace. Also, it is well to remember that Peter says that it is only through this state of suffering that a saint is able to reach the highest level of Christian experience (1 Peter 5:10). In this state of suffering, saints of God learn that the greatest value is humbly to bow before the throne of God and seek the assistance of the sovereign Lord (Romans 12:12).

It was while enduring these times of great suffering that my mother cried many bitter tears over my life and my state of retardation. It was at this time that God placed her tears into a bottle as a memorial of God's grace that would be poured out upon me. Remember David! David said, "Put thou my tears into a bottle" (Psalms 56:8)!

It was during these times that she lived this expression, "O eyes, no eyes, but fountains fraught with tears! O Life, no life, but lively form of death!" It was out of these times that she knew, "out of the presses of pain cometh the soul's best wine and the eyes which shed no tears can shed but little shine and glory!"

It was due to her tears that God was touched to move. These tears became the backbone of the ministry that was to come forth. Her tears nourished this ministry and gave birth to it. It was prophesied, "Every tear that she sowed in prayer was a seed, which the Lord received that will bring forth a millionfold blessing and harvest that God will produce in the ministry!" Tertullian once said that the blood of the martyrs nourished the church. So have this ministry and my life been nourished by the tears of my mother. The Psalmist said, "They that sow in tears shall reap in joy. He that goeth forth and weepeth, bearing precious seed, shall doubtless come again with rejoicing, bringing his sheaves with him" (Psalms 126:5).

It has been said that all men are moved to pray with deep feeling and emotion and even to tears. Tears are the sign that something is breaking up our emotions. Tears also refresh and clean the very inner man. The Bible may be said to be "a theology of tears." A. W. Tozer once said, "The Bible was written in tears and to tears it will yield its best treasure." How true! Too often within the Bible, the tears of the saints are seen to be at the forefront. It was the tears of Hezekiah that touched God and moved God to heal him (2 Kings 20:1). Notice that Hezekiah mixed his prayers with tears and found acceptance. David said that his tears were his meat day and night (Psalms 42:3).

A telescope is nothing when compared to the tears of the saints. Telescopes can only see the countless stars. On the other hand, godly tears reach out to those things that are unknown and reveal things for which no telescope was ever made.

Tears are the literal reflections of our inner man. They are pieces of our memories, our own hurts, and our own experiences. In reality, tears (that are shed by the saints) are the very dying out of our own selves (Psalms 42:3; 56:8 126:5; Acts 20:19; 2 Kings 20:5). When God speaks to us, we expect God to move not now but yesterday. The problem is that God does not always work as fast as we want Him to work. Why? Sometimes, God will heavily test our faith. In these times, we must stand and stand upon our faith, holding on when there is no hope. We must be like the patriarchs and the other saints of the Old Testament times, believing and holding on whether we ever receive or not (Hebrews 11:1-13).

Tears are seen, by God, as signs of trust. In other words, God sees tears as signs that we trust Him for our home, lives, and all possessions. Tears are seen, by God, as that most glorious sign that we are surrendering to Him. They are seen as the bursting forth of total surrender to a merciful God.

The ministries of the Prophets and the Apostles were founded upon their tears. Their tears effected what they thundered in words. Without the shedding of tears, the Prophets and the Apostles could not have touched the very throne of God for assistance, nor could they have been commissioned for their missions.

The early saints saw tears as a sign of repentance, and a cleansing agent of the Lord. The tears the woman cried out for Jesus in Matthew 26:7-15 were a sign of her repentance and sorrow. To the early saints, tears were beseeching the Lord with travailing and with repentance. The early saints believed that, with lamentation and tears, a person could touch the heart of the Lord most of all when nothing else could. They saw that the tears of Hezekiah were the root cause that moved God to extend his life; above all things God saw tears shed (2 Kings 20:1). They saw that when two or more saints shed tears over a believer, Christ also sheds tears, and He prays for mercy. They believed that when faithful tears are shed from eyes that have looked upon wickedness, they satisfy God. Finally, they held that tears were sent forth as ambassadors to God for our sufferings.

The Jews believe that the tears of the Jewish women touched God more than anything else in moving to set free the Jewish nation from Pharaoh. These tears turned God's face toward the Jewish people when before due to their sin, He had turned His face away. It was not the tears of the men but the tears of the women that touched God.

Often my mother said that she believed she cried a river of tears stretching from Jacksonville to Fernandina. She turned the time of commuting to work into her praying time. Consequently, the title of this book is, *A Walk through Tears.* It was this precious time that touched the heart of God, just as David so sought after the very heart of God (1 Samuel 13:14).

Someone once said, "God is not the God over troubled waters but the God through troubled waters." It is God who carries us through the storms of life. It is He who shines forth showers of blessings and deliverances, following a bitter, dry famine. God will pull us through all these storms if we can withstand the pull. The pulling of God brings pain and anguish because we do not understand what God wants. But, through all of this, we can gain the victory over the storms if we learn to be more like Christ and less what we are. After all, the philosophy of the cross is, "We must decrease and He must increase."

So often during these bitter tears, my mother would wonder, "Has God forsaken us?" or "Where is God?" Yet, God, in the midst of these storms, was there, never forsaking us nor abandoning us. We have the promise from the Word that God will never leave us nor forsake us (Hebrew 13:5). We can depend upon His promises. God cannot lie! Though God seems far away, the truth can be only that He has not left us. Deliverance will come, but it may take longer than we want. Deliverance comes in God's timing, never in our own timing (Ecclesiastes 3; Psalms

34:19). If we forget that, it will bring destruction upon our lives, for we will blame God for our failures.

Even David himself in Psalm 22:1 said, "My God, my God, Why has thou forsaken me?" From this, it is learned that there are many seasons when the dark clouds of suffering always eclipse the brightness of our Father's smile, and it appears that we stand alone without the Father.

A 19th poet, Fredirck W. Faber, expressed very well the seeming absence of God in times of troubles:

He hides Himself so wondrously
As though there were no God;
He is least seen when all the powers
of ill are most abroad.
Or He deserts us at the hour
The fight is almost lost.
And seems to leave us to ourselves
Just when we need Him most
It is not so, but so it looks;
And we lose courage then;
And doubts will come if God hath kept
His promise to men.

Therefore, cry out to that God of the miraculous as our whole family did. Beseech Him to touch the untouchable or those that appear to have no hope. God is the God of the hopeless as I truly was a hopeless case. Please remember our family motto, "We would rather believe and not receive than could have believed and could have received." We held on, not giving in, not giving up, and not giving out. We held onto the promises of God, mentioned in the Bible, regarding healing and miracles. We had simple and uneducated faith that those promises are valid today, and we did whatever God demanded of us. God demands that we reach up to Him so He can reach down to us!

1

THE EARLY LIFE OF MY HUSBAND

My husband, George Elias Roberts, and I were raised very similarly. In fact, we lived just twenty miles apart from each other. Both our families worked as farmers during the Great Depression.

My husband was born premature and not supposed to live. Why? It was due to the inadequacy of hospitals, money, lack of proper equipment, and medicine during this terrible period of American history. He was born so premature that it was said, "his bed was a shoe box." His sister also remarked that the wedding ring of his mother would fit up to his elbow. Because of this premature birth, he had to be watched twenty-four hours a day, had to be kept at a very warm temperature, and had to be fed with an eyedropper. These circumstances were difficult because the house that the family lived in was old, cold and drafty, had many holes through the walls, and had only a lonely fireplace as heat.

Since almost everyone around Coffee County, Georgia had lost their possessions during the Great Depression, it was very fortunate for a family to have any type of food on the table and a place to live, much less to have a doctor. If any town did have a doctor, he would be paid usually with bacon, ham, or chickens. Nevertheless, most of the poor families were medically treated by old remedies that might or might not work.

The circumstances of those difficult times were no different for Elias, though it helped that his grandmother Lanie was a midwife. Since his grandmother Lanie had seen so many babies born prematurely who did not live, she knew that he would need a miracle to survive. Grandmother Lanie was a prayer-warrior. Grandmother Lanie was also a jack of all trades. She was a midwife, a prayer-warrior, and a retailer selling eggs and other things grown on the farm. Boy! She could do a little preaching too! She was the one who taught my mother-in-law how to pray.

Many godly men and women living in the Great Depression found time to pray all night. They also found time to fast during these hard times. Let it be said that through these times, with so many worldly possessions having been lost, their faith, their Christian walk, and their Christian talk with God never deterred once. In essence, the hard times made them stronger in their faith while others were financially and spiritually collapsing all around. Many became shipwrecked in their faith, and yet by the grace of God, others found their faith. Still others persevered in their faith, never giving in, never giving up, and never giving out. Glory to the Most High God!

Elias was very sickly for most of his life. In times past, he would describe having the worst swimming headaches that any person could ever imagine when he talked about himself as a little boy. These types of headaches are similar to migraines but with some medical differences. Elias often talked about carrying water in a bucket to his father, while his father was in the field working, and having these headaches begin anew. When this took place, he would actually see the field turning round and round and would often throw up. In these times of great distress, his father would find Elias so sick that Elias could

2

not pick up his own head and would have to be carried back to the house.

Thank God for praying saints! The family had a neighbor known as "Jumping Jim Carter." This man had an ice-route. One day Jim Carter found Elias sick with a swimming headache when he came to deliver ice. Mrs. Roberts asked Brother Carter if he had time to pray for Elias. His answer was, "I always have time to pray for someone who's sick." After Brother Carter prayed for Elias, he never had another swimming headache again.

Just as God in His infinite mercy touched Elias and delivered him from those horrible headaches through Brother Carter's prayer, so God allowed Elias to be instrumental in laying the foundation for Brother Carter's great great grandson to be saved fifty years later.

So often Satan tried his best to kill or injure Elias. When he was seven or eight-years-old, his oldest brother, J.H., carried him down to a water hole to go swimming. Elias, thinking that it would be all right to jump in, jumped and landed on a log underneath the water causing severe damage and pain to his lower back. The damage and pain were so severe that when J.H. looked at him he thought that Elias was dead. J.H. believed that Elias had broken his back. It took some time before Elias could walk again. For the rest of his life God often healed him. However, God never healed him of this. Yet, Elias never allowed this pain to get the better of him. Many days he worked like a dog in pain to provide for our family.

As Charles Dickens once said, "It was the best of times; it was the worst of times." Our parents did not think that education was important. They taught us how to work and that was the only education that they believed we needed. Dealing with this attitude of prejudice against education, Elias was forced to remain uneducated and had to go to work on a farm to make a living. Though his for-

3

mal education only extended through the third-grade, he had a head full of common sense. I believe that he was able to learn. Yet, I believe that Satan stole from him the opportunity to study and to be well-rounded. What greatness and glory Satan stole from him! If people had been more learned in spiritual-warfare (back then as they are now), some would have stood up against the plans and devices of Satan.

Remember what Jesus said about Satan and later himself, "The thief cometh not, but for to steal, and to kill, and to destroy; I am come that they might have life, and that they might have it more abundantly" (John 10:10). Notice that Christ says here that the saints can have life more abundantly. In Elias' early life, Satan stole many things from him. This could not have been due to sin. It must have been due to a lack of knowledge. In other words, no one was teaching the Word of God as it must be taught at least around that area. Neither were friends or their family able to attend much church and learn the means to fight Satan. When they would go to church, they would either go in a mule drawn wagon or walk through the woods in the late hours of the night. Therefore, their concern was not so much about how to fight Satan as it was to survive.

The Word of God says, "My people are destroyed for lack of knowledge: because thou has rejected knowledge, I will also reject thee, that shalt be no priest to me: seeing thou has forgotten the law of thy God, I will also forget thy children" (Hosea 4:6). The rejection of knowledge, in particular the rejection of godly knowledge, will destroy people. Knowledge and an education that are well-rounded and well-grounded upon the Word of God will bring life and bring deliverance. They will each enter the territory of darkness, bring life, bring deliverance, and destroy the devilish plans of darkness.

Satan repeatedly wins not by force but in particular by deception and by his victims' ignorance of how to fight against him and his evil forces. Paul himself said, "Lest Satan should get an advantage of us: for we are not ignorant of his devices" (2 Corinthians 2:11). The devices of Satan must be learned from the Scriptures, the Spirit, and experience. We must not be ignorant of Satan and his devices. If we are ignorant, we will reap nothing good but everything evil and destructive. Guard yourself from ignorance of Satan's devices and of God's Word! Know that as soon as one battle ends another begins. Satan never gives up fighting against a saint. The Christian walk is filled with battles ending and battles beginning.

Nevertheless, praise the Lord, Elias was able to hold down jobs. In fact, he worked forty-one years on the same job but for different companies as a corrugator operator (which is one who operates a machine that makes cardboard boxes). God had given him so much common sense that he could hear the machine running and could tell what was wrong with it. For this ability he was named, "Mister Corrugator of America." This entitled him to be offered a job with a large company doing much traveling, going about installing the corrugators, and teaching others how to use this very large machine.

Elias was the greatest Father in the world. His son and our family were more important to him than anything in the world. He knew that I could not raise Ricky, our son, alone. Therefore, he had to reject this wonderful job. Yet, he did not regret rejecting this offer. Why? From the time that Ricky was born, until he was six- years-old, Ricky slept in our bed under Elias' arm. Why? Because if we went to sleep, and Ricky had a convulsion, Elias would know what was wrong or what was going on. So often Elias would wake me up to get a spoon and put it upon

Ricky's tongue. Then, Elias and I knew that we were on the way to the hospital with Ricky again.

Elias was the kind of man who is unselfish and puts his child first in all things, except before the Lord. This means that Elias would willingly get up and cook something for Ricky to eat when Ricky became hungry in the night. The reason for this was that Ricky was very sickly in his early years, and when Ricky wanted something to eat, we decided to give it to him. To us, the hunger of Ricky was a sign that he was all right.

Elias never became too tired to carry Ricky to kindergarten or to a tutor, to cook, to wash, and to take care of Ricky for me when I had to work. He was familiar with the working of the house, and he relieved me of much responsibility. Some of the best times that I remember were when we cooked, gardened and canned fresh vegetables together. This manner of life came from how he helped his mother when he was young. His mother often said that he would never leave her while she was still canning. He would stay with her no matter the day, the hour, or the circumstance. The kitchen would have to be cleaned completely so that when he sat down, she could sit down too.

If there is such a thing as a godly seed, I believe that it was placed in Elias from the beginning because he was always a family man. He loved his home and family.

His mother said, "Elias never gave me a bit of trouble." He was kind and gentle. The only time that she could remember him giving her any trouble was in his early years. Before he was saved, he decided to drink moonshine, which made him very drunk. He tried to slip up the steps to his room without her knowing it. But she noticed that he did not wash his feet. Every night, from the time he was a little boy, he would be sure to take a bath and then wash his feet before retiring. Yet, this night

6

he did not take a bath or wash his feet but slipped up to bed. When she came into his room and found out that he was drunk, she woke him up and had a long talk with him. This conversation alone was enough to make him never want to drink again. In other words, she shamed him, and it worked. From this, it is easy to see how God had been preparing him for the life that was before him.

As I remember, Elias was a man who truly loved children. He loved not only ours but all children. When we would go to Georgia on a visit, we would take the nephews and nieces fishing and hunting. If the nephews wanted the game cooked at three or four o'clock in the morning, he would clean and cook it for the children. When they all went hunting, he taught them the right way to use a shotgun or any other type of firearm. At my husband's funeral one nephew said that Elias could have had fifty children and enjoyed every one of them.

Elias had four brothers and one sister. When his oldest brother brought Elias to my house (when I was eight-years-old), Elias said, "I will marry that girl, Dot." He told me that day how I was dressed. I was dressed in a blue shirt and overalls; I also had my hair cut short. I surely made an impression upon him although he was eleven years of age! I wish, dear God, I knew what I did! I just do not remember him at that age. He must not have made a very good impression upon me. However, later, he surely did! How do I know? I married him!

From afar, he watched me grow up. I had a blind date with him, well-sort of. I was in Douglas one Saturday when my girlfriend came up and asked whether I would go out with her and her boyfriend, who was a cousin of Elias. The purpose was so that I would date Elias. Knowing the purpose, I said at first, "No! I do not date anyone I do not know." Yet, I changed my mind. That night we went to a theater and dated a few times later. For that reason, he easily accepted that we were going steady when I knew nothing about it. Then, he left town.

When he came back to town, I was not the same young woman that he left, but I was a new person. During his absence, I had met Jesus. From that time on I only dated boys who attended the Church of God. Elias had no problem with that. In fact, we became hard workers for the Lord. We would pick up young people and carry them to church with us. Our local preacher was so impressed with us that he preached a sermon called "Working for the Lord." He dedicated it to both Elias and me.

THE EARLY LIFE OF MY FAMILY

Before my mother ever thought of my father, he had been married. Here came the tragedy! My father had been married for some time to a cherished lady, Lillie. She had given him a child, a girl, and was carrying the second child when the tragedy took place. The disaster that struck our family was a murder. My father's first wife was murdered very brutally by a man whom my father had known and trusted for a considerable time. By the good graces of my father and another farmer this man, who was to become a murderer, was released from the chain gang. Within ten days of his release he murdered Lillie while my father and a farm-worker were working out in the field. The brutality of this murder shocked the whole community. This type of murder was unheard of at this time in Georgia.

The fiendishness of the murder was so great that it disturbingly shook the whole nation on May 22, 1918. It was nationally reported in the Associated Press and national newspapers. The Cordelle Dispatch reported on the murder, and wrote:

> Mrs. Simmons was a small woman, but she was not frail. If there was the slightest resistance to the brute attack, there was no evidence left. The dining room, stove, and a table containing the cooking things in the small cook room were in their place and not disordered. If anything was

9

thrown to the floor in a scuffle, it had been re-
placed by the fiend. Only two bloody table forks
were found in the yard. The bludgeon with which
Mrs. Simmons head was battered to a pulp with
was nowhere to be found....Further, Mrs.
Simmons was attacked with forks. She was
stabbed so often with the fork attack that the top
of a pepper duster could not have possibly contained more perforations. The forks were both
bent up in the attack so as to render them useless in a further assault of this character. This
stabbing with the forks indicated that the murderer thought thus to reach her heart and end
her life. But the bludgeon was apparently later
used and as many as five or six terrible stroked
were plainly apparent in the different apertures
in her head on the right side in the temple and
over the right eye. Her sewing was still under
the needle of her machine on the front porch of
the house. Her shoes were in the room adjoin-
ing the kitchen. She laid in her stocking feet, her
dress and underwear partially stripped away
from her neck and right shoulder, but still pinned
with two safety pins. About her throat were slight
signs that she may have first been choked into
insensibility, and around her, the blood from her
body had flowed directly across the room. Her
brains were shattered and scattered to the walls
of the kitchen by the powerful strokes of the
implement of death used by the brute....

The untold shock of the horrifying experience of finding his wife murdered and seeing his first child crawling
in the blood of her dead mother left unimaginable scars
and baggage on my father that just could not be healed in
any way that man could have developed. Only if my fa-

ther had gone to a preacher, or to a pastor baptized with the Holy Spirit and empowered with the spiritual gifts of the Holy Spirit, could he have found peace. It is the baptism of the Holy Spirit and the spiritual gifts that release the power of God to set people free. Remember that Psalms 55:22 says, "Cast thy burden upon the Lord, and he will sustain thee: He will never suffer the righteous to be moved."

The problem, however, was that my father was not saved! If he had been saved, this horrifying tragedy might never have taken place. If only he had walked in the arms of Jesus throughout all his life, this murder might not have seen the light of day, nor would he have had to carry this burden until he was seventy-five years old (when he was saved by the Lord Jesus Christ). If he had only confessed with his mouth the Lord Jesus and believed with his heart in his early life, he would have received divine help.

After the murder and before my father married his second wife, my mother, something strange and demonic took place in his life. It began very simply. He had a new horse and a new buggy, and he was traveling by a cemetery near dusk. As he approached the cemetery, he stopped the buggy and the horse, stepped out of the buggy, and began to walk the horse for a time. The very stopping of my father by the cemetery was out of the ordinary. While he had stopped horses many times to give them a rest, he never stopped by a cemetery. He was raised to fear the demonic activity, instead of believing that the blood of Christ, the name of Jesus, the death of Christ, and the cross are protection from it. Because of his fear, he did not go near a cemetery since it was believed that the demonic resides there. He would travel far from anything like that.

All things seemed all right at the cemetery until my father saw something gray that resembled a small dog

11

such as a poodle. There were no dogs like that where my father lived in Georgia.

Instead of fleeing the cemetery and this phenomenon of the supernatural, he ran after it and tried to pick it up. I do not know how long my father continued trying to grasp this apparition. Nevertheless, I do know that it disappeared, and he could not find it again. I believe that this apparition was a demon spirit resembling the form of a dog. The reason I believe this is because after this event my father was never the same. It was as if something had possessed him, and it was not holy, good, or righteous. I believe that he became demon-possessed.

Why would this apparition entice my father to follow it? For his destruction! Do not the Scriptures warn all humanity about trafficking with demon spirits (Leviticus 19:11; 20:6; Deuteronomy 18:11; 1 Samuel 28:7-25; 2 Kings. 21:6; 23:24; 1 Chronicles 10:13; 2 Chronicles 33:6; Isaiah 8:19; 19:3; 29:4)? Now, my father did this in ignorance, but others do it intentionally. The only protection against demon-possession is the blood of Christ, the name of Jesus, the death of Christ, and the cross.

My mother came into the picture about three years later. When she appeared in my father's life, she married a man already having a family. Not once can I remember my mother complaining about her mother-in-law or about her stepchild. It seems from all evidence that she loved her stepchild as her own. His family and the family of his first wife were always welcomed in our house. Finding the Father of my father's first wife on our farm was very common. There was no contention between the families. All tried their best to get along, and all tried their best to make a living or what can be called a living.

My mother was a great woman, strong, well-rounded, well-meaning, determined, hard working and homebound. If she had not been, the marriage would have failed. In later years, my mother became so home-bound in her old home place that when my father built her a new house, her children had to go and move her out. She did not want to go, but she succumbed to all the wills of her children. She centered her life around her family and her home.

As I said before, both my husband and I were raised on farms. There were six girls and just one boy in my family. Before World War II, and especially through the Great Depression, my father worked outside the farm, and my mother hired men to help her work on the farm. It was often said that my father would work all day selling groceries, catch a train home at twelve or one o'clock at night, and then walk about five miles with a sack filled with groceries that contained nothing but essentials. The essentials meant those things that could not be grown on the farm, such as salt, flour, coffee, and other useful things.

I am sorry to say that by the time I was born, the damaging effects of my father's past life had already taken a heavy toll on what remained of his life. Those consequences of his life led him into a life of rebellion, drunkenness, and debauchery.

These ungodly manifestations were foreign to his upbringing and how he had lived his life before the time of sorrow had crept into his life. Before this time, my father had been a well-known baseball player. My father-in-law remarked that he had seen my father many times pitch in baseball games. Further, according to my father, he said that during this time he had worked in some capacity with the federal government. However, all this time, he still continued to work on his own farm.

My father began drinking when he was no longer working with the federal government but with the state government of Georgia. He was a sinner; yet, he was not known to drink. My father-in-law said that my father never drank any thing stronger than soda until the latter years.

What began this road of destruction can be blamed in part to his participating in cocktail parties after closing. This taste of sin led him into deeper depths of sin. I believe that if he had any idea that this could have robbed him of his dignity and hurt his family, he would have never begun sipping. Too many saints follow this slippery path back into sin and depravity. Paul himself warns in 1 Corinthians 6:9-10 and 1 Corinthians 9:27, just to name two passages, that sin is death. The most famous passage is where Paul says, "For the wages of sin is death; but the gift of God is eternal life through Jesus Christ our Lord" (Romans 6:23). My father truly tasted the wages of sin! Yet, praise God, five years before he died, he tasted the Shechinah Glory–the divine presence of the Lord and the loving grace of God when he received the gift of eternal life!

Salvation of a soul is what counts after all. It counts more than anything else does–more than life, more than fame, and more than money. Thank God my father woke up before it was too late! How many today will never wake up to this reality? The precious Gospel is reaching down to the sinners and calling out for their deliverance and their salvation. All that is required for any sinner to do is to reach out to that great salvation that awaits him. Please, run to that altar of repentance, be reconciled back to God, and allow God to be reconciled back to you!

By the time I was six- years-old, my mother was leading three of her children in the field, plowing, planting, and breaking up unploughed ground. No matter how cold or hot it was, we had to work. Our survival depended, in the later years, upon the farm. It sustained us in the worst of times. My mother was both a supercook and a superfarmer. She could teach anyone how to work on a farm. I have seen her countless times pick cotton so fast that it would bewilder the mind. It had been said that she and the children could pick a full bale of cotton in two days. She also enjoyed picking butter beans. During this time, my father, being an alcoholic, was very little help on the farm.

Turning our attention toward her cooking, it must be said that if anyone had eaten a meal that she cooked, he or she would have never forgotten it. She never knew how many would be sitting at our table on a given day. People would invite themselves into her home and feel welcomed. After working for some time in the field, Mother would leave her work, go into the kitchen, and begin to cook lunch or dinner. When the children would come to eat, there would always be plenty of food; sometimes, there would even be a churn of ice cream or old fashion tea-cakes. We worked hard, and we ate very well. I also remember my mother going into a cold kitchen and cooking a large breakfast with homemade biscuits, homemade butter, and homemade syrup. I have so many wonderful memories of my mother; yet, I would never want those days to come back!

In later years, my mother's health began to fail and that put more work on the children, especially on me after my sister married. When we came home from school, it was common for us to pick a wagon load of cucumbers to take to the market. We would take the wagon down by the rail road track at night and hope that no train would come and frighten the mule and make him spill the cucumbers that we wanted to sell. We had to try to keep the mule calm. We needed as many cucumbers as we could get because the trips to the market gave my father extra money.

Though times were hard and money was not easy to come by when we would take our goods to market, both my father and mother always allowed us to buy what we wanted to eat. Most of the time, we children would buy RC Cola and cinnamon buns and charge the items to my father's account. As long as we did not waste the money or buy things he would not approve of, my father did not care what we bought. We knew what to buy and what not to buy. If we bought something that my father disapproved of, we would be punished. However, we had to work for the money to buy our own clothes for school and for anything else.

All the children knew what it was to dip turpentine, to cut trees down for wood, to sit up all night to fire a tobacco barn, and to crop tobacco the next morning. The mules always had to be fed, and the cows had to be attended. There was never time for rest, for prayer, or for God. We always had something to do. My father was as good as gold when he was not drinking, and he would help anyone who was less fortunate than we were. Yet when he would drink, a force would take over his life and personality. In essence, he would take on a split personality, like Doctor Jekyll and Mister Hyde. When he would drink, he would brutally beat us. He never knew when he needed to stop. It was quite easy for him to believe, "Spare not the rod" (Proverbs 22:15; 23:13; 29:15). He beat us so much when he was drunk that, on occasion, blood would flow from our backs.

The last time I remember my father whipping me when he was drinking was with a tobacco stick. I received this beating because I could not plow a watermelon patch planted in a rocky field, which had not received any rain for a considerable time. When he whipped me on this occasion, I refused to cry. This made him very angry. He continued to hit me harder and unmercifully. Thank God my mother walked outside and saw what was going on! She ran to him, took away the tobacco stick, shouted to him, "You are going to kill her!" and finally he stopped. I was a young teenager that time and, I warned him that would be the last time he would beat me or ever lay his hands on me again. The next day he was very sorrowful over the whole incident especially since he himself could not plow the same piece of field.

So often I remember my father leaving the house to go to town. I would wonder whether he was going to come back home drunk or sober. Due to his drunkenness and the horrible beatings the other children and I suffered, I often prayed to God as a child that my father would die before he came home. Yet, I prayed this as a little child, innocent, and not yet saved by the blood of Christ. Later, I thanked God that He knew best and did not grant my petition! As I think back to those days, many families were dysfunctional according to the standards of today.

We were not a religious family, but when we did go to church, we had to walk because we didn't have a car. However, in these early years, I would see my mother have the faith to believe that it would rain before it would be too late to save the crops. The rains would come due to her faith. She always held this faith and was never disappointed. Even my father was never too drunk to pray grace over his meal.

In these early years, God did not abandon my family, nor me. On one cold day when I was about five years of age, my overalls caught fire, and the fire burned my leg so bad that my parents thought I would never walk again. But, thank God, a preacher was running a revival close to our house and was blessed with the power of the Holy Spirit upon his life! He came into my house and prayed for my leg. In a few days I was walking. God completely healed my leg.

I remember once at Easter my brother and I walked to church. The Sunday School teacher at the church happened to be a lady who helped us put in tobacco. The next time we worked together she remarked that if everyone came all the time as people did on Easter or Christmas the church would be filled. My remark back to her was that she was my Sunday School teacher, and there was no difference between us. Why? She smoked and cursed like I did. She smoked publicly; I smoked slipping around where my parents would not know. If they had known, I would have had hell to pay. This conversation between us caused my teacher to judge herself and accept the Lord as her Savior. Then, there was a difference, a good difference. In fact, she became very peculiar to me. Do not the Scriptures say that the saints of God are a peculiar people (1 Peter 2:9)? Notice that she was teaching the Word of God and yet was not saved. How many are either teaching or preaching the Word of God and are not saved? Many people going to hell are those who are present at church and have never yet known that glorious relationship with Christ.

In a particular Church of God, there was a lady with whom my father had a sexual affair. This took place a long time before she was saved and a long time before she attended this church. My first strike against that particular Church of God was that she attended it. I was hurt over the affair. The affair caused untold troubles in our family and especially to my mother. Extramarital affairs such as this always bring nothing but heartache, destruction, and death.

Knowing this lady, I often swore that when I was grown, I would beat her senseless. I always remarked that if that church allowed women of whoredom to go there, I did not want any part of that church.

I did not realize that long after that affair had ended, the Lord Jesus had saved her, and she had become a new creation in Christ Jesus. There is a difference between the old you and the new you when Christ comes into your life. If not, there is no true conversion at all.

One other strike against this church can be described as out of the ordinary. I had never been around Pentecostal churches. I had never seen what in the world went on there. I had never seen the shouting, the strange utterances of tongues, the healings, the miracles, and the other manifestations of the Holy Spirit. The very first time I ever experienced hearing these strange utterances of tongues, or ever heard a shout of praise, was a shocking experience. As it happens, I spent one night with my Aunt Hazel and my cousin. Since they only had one bedroom, I (as a young teenager) had to sleep between both of them. About four o'clock in the morning, I was awakened by the strange and awful commotion of my aunt jumping, shouting, and speaking something strange, which I had never heard in my life. I believe that my hair actually stood up. I ran behind my cousin, and said, "If she gets me, she has to get you first!" When Aunt Hazel began to calm down, she lifted her hands in the air, walked into the kitchen, and all that I could hear her say was something like, "I thank the ghost." From childhood, my family and I would sit around the fire and, on occasion, we would hear all sorts of ghost stories. So, I was ready to leave that place. If there were not a door, I was ready to make a door. When she walked back into the bedroom, I heard her plainly thanking the "Holy Ghost" and praising God for His visitation. As she was thanking the Lord, I was looking around to see if I could see the Lord, too. Finally, the manifestation of the Holy Spirit subsided. My aunt said, "Kids, we can go back to bed now." I pointed my finger at my cousin, and said, "This time, you sleep beside her!"

Often I heard my aunt say that she wanted to leave this world shouting and speaking in tongues. That is just what happened. God granted her desire.

19

One night as I was attending that same church of God, not by choice, a lady preacher, Sister Mae Terry, was the guest speaker. Her sermon was not a sermon made for itching ears (2 Tim. 4:3), nor was it a sermon filled only with empty words. Her sermon was a sermon of power.

In these later years, it reminds me of the sermon preached by Jonathan Edwards. The sermon was called "Sinners in the Hands of an Angry God." When Jonathan Edwards preached this sermon, the hearers felt hell and its torments round about them. So much conviction was wrought by this sermon that hundreds would run to the altar to be saved. Jonathan Edwards would continue to preach this sermon to new hearers. This sermon never became old or outdated because it had the fire of God within it.

Just like the sermon that Jonathan Edwards preached so long ago, Sister Mae Terry preached a hell, fire, and brimstone sermon. I personally believed that the seat I was sitting on was on fire when she gave the altar call. At first, all I remember was that somehow I found myself down at the altar crying out to Jesus to save my soul. The next thing I remember was that a woman was behind me praying and she had her hand upon my back. Her hand felt like a warm iron. I turned around to see just who she was that had her hand upon my back and saw the woman whom I had hated because of her having a sexual affair with my father. That night God burned all the bitterness and hatred that I had held for years against her. I truly became that new creation in Christ Jesus that Paul speaks of in 2 Corinthians 5:17. All the baggage that I had in my life melted away. The effects of my dysfunctional family were washed away by the blood of Christ, which is truly sufficient. If not, then salvation is an illusion.

That night, as a young teenager, I met and fell in love with Jesus. That type of love I knew nothing about and was not going to give it up, whatever the cost. If there were not enough tears already shed, there would be much more shedding of tears in the coming years for my son and for my family. I had no idea just how much I was going to need Jesus in the coming years. I could neither imagine the pain nor the anguish that I would also endure.

When I was saved that night, the Church of God did not take it too seriously. They saw the type of family I was born into and concluded that I would never make it. Still, I want all the saints to know that the Bible says, "He which hath begun a good work in you will perform it until the day of Jesus Christ" (Philippians 1:6). That has been proven in my life!

While I was pure sexually before I married and even before I was saved, the saving of my soul enforced my belief and conviction to remain a virgin until marriage and to date boys who had found the same Savior that I had.

When I was saved that night, I began a life of intercessory prayer for my family. At this time, no one in my family was saved. I was the baby girl and the only one standing in the gap for my family. Thank God the next persons who were saved in my family were my sister and brother-in-law! She was a little older than I was. So often I have wondered just who prayed for our salvation.

For years the life and practice of intercessory prayer for my family (and especially for my father) did not bear much fruit that I could see. In fact, circumstances of life became worse. My father began to drink more instead of less. From this, I have learned that when a saint intercedes for his or her family, he or she is in a battle for the very souls of all concerned, and the very battle may not bear very much fruit for a time. It may have been easier if there had been books on intercessory prayer back then.

Even if that had been the case, we would not have had the money to buy them anyway. Therefore, all I could do was believe that the Lord would lead me every step of the way. I really did not know how to pray. Yet, I would find a place in a field and cry out to God, learning how to pray in stages. I would pray on the school bus, walking, and even in my bed. In the bed I would take my pillow, put it over my head, cry, and pray myself to sleep.

In my early Christian experience, I was in great travail, during a particular Sunday, over my family. I went down to the altar praying and the burden over my family was so heavy that I felt I could not bear it. So, I left the altar and went to my Sunday School class. In the room by myself, I began to cry out to God for help. The Lord gave me a vision and told me that if I would serve Him, He would save my family and especially my father. After I came out of the vision, I looked and saw my Aunt Hazel praying with me. That night the Lord did not tell me that I would have to wait twenty years before my father would be saved. Neither did God tell me that for twenty years when I would go home, I would see my father dog-drunk and his arteries on his neck so enlarged that they looked as if they were about to explode. All during this time, I did not know whether he would have a stroke or kill someone in a drunken state. God simply said that my father would be saved. All God gave me was a piece of a puzzle, not all the pieces of that puzzle. It would have been very simple for God to have given me all the pieces. But where would my faith have been?

All during the twenty years my father's condition did not get any better but became worse and worse, as is the case for most alcoholics. Later there would only be a few days that he would not be drinking. But even these days were terrible. How? As an alcoholic, he was suffering the symptoms of what is known as "withdrawal." During these times, it was very common for him to have hallucinations of elephants, pink rats running up the wall, and other images. Finally, my mother had enough and put him in a hospital where he could receive help for his alcoholism. But at the time he was not ready for help. The demons of hell made him angrier when he was in that hospital. When he finally left the hospital, he went back to the same type of life that mother and the children had hoped the hospital would resolve somehow.

After a little while I went home and carried both my mother and my father to town so that they could see about the tobacco that they had on the market to sell. That Saturday morning, as any other day, anyone could tell that he had been drinking. I did not let on that I knew he had been drinking whiskey. I said, "Dad, you have been good today. I know that you want a drink. Where do you buy your whiskey? It is time that this family owns up that we have an alcoholic father and not be ashamed of it anymore." I gave him twenty dollars and carried him to get a bottle of whiskey. When he came out of the whiskey store, I said to him, "Is that enough to last till Monday?" I did not want him to be on the road and kill some innocent person. His remark to me was, "Now, let us not over do this d— thing!" I said to him, "We have tried to get help for you to quit drinking with no success. The God that you serve is the god of alcoholism. When you die, I am going to put a fifth of whiskey in your coffin, for that fifth of whiskey is the god that you are going to hell for, for all eternity!" He was ready for help Monday morning. The hospital this time made it hard on him. The medical staff put him in with mental patients that had severe problems. Such were the problems of these mental patients that my father was frightened for his very life. He prayed that if God would let him live, he would serve Him and never drink again. At that moment, my father was saved. His

23

last testimony before his death was, "Since I have found the Master, I have found no detour signs." The preacher preached this message at my father's funeral.

God was not finished with our family and had not yet fulfilled His entire promise to me about my family. The saving of my father was a great part of that. Yet, other parts were to be fulfilled. One by one, my family began to come into the fullness of the Lord. Thank the Lord for His mercy and grace. Thank God He brings to pass what He promises, as long as you do your part! The last person of my family that God promised to save came to the Lord only two years before the writing of this book.

3

BATTLING FOR A MIRACLE

While the spiritual warfare for my family began long before the battle for my son, the focus of this chapter can only be the battle fought for my son. The battle to receive a miracle for my son can be really seen to have begun even before his birth and even before I was married. The Lord was preparing me and warning me that there would be a battle.

Elias and I prayed earnestly for about a year to be married. We were married in 1951 and soon afterward moved down to Jacksonville, FL. Having no money, and only a small job that paid very little, we made this unheard of move from everything that we knew. Unaware that God was moving us out of our safety zone, we found ourselves in Jacksonville in miserable conditions. We barely survived for two years. We hardly ate anything during this period. The only thing that we could afford was cabbage and grits day in and day out. It is amazing to me that even now I still enjoy eating cabbage and grits. After God saw that He could trust us with what we had, He gave us better jobs and helped us save some money.

Even before I received a very good job, I relentlessly prayed that God would give me a good job. I told Him that I would never use it selfishly. When Elias and I would go to church, people would always look us up and down. Why? At this time, money was very scarce, and we did not have the money to buy expensive clothes. Even Elias would walk to work to save gas so that we could go to church. One night we decided to go to a church near our home. The preacher saw that I had no stockings on and preached against me not wearing them.

Easter would come and go. I would have to wear the same old dresses that I had been wearing during the week. Finally, the Lord gave me a very good job, and Easter was on its way. I began to put money back, dollar by dollar, to buy that expensive Easter outfit. I had saved a hundred and fifty dollars.

I had planned to go shopping the Saturday before Easter. However, the Lord had not forgotten my promise to Him at all, although it had been months since I made that promise. That Wednesday, the Lord led me to a particular home. At that home, I found an elderly woman and her disabled son. Both the woman and her son were very sick and had been to the doctor. However, they had no money to buy medicine or food. The cabinets were empty, and they had not eaten for days, nor did they have any gas with which to cook.

I carried the prescriptions to a pharmacy and ran to the grocery store. In the grocery store, I was just going to spend enough money to buy a little food for them. In other words, I was going to buy them only the cheap things and just enough so that they could survive.

As I was walking down the aisles, I will never forget the Lord speaking to me. He said in very simple words, "Feed them as you want Me to feed you." I do not know whether power brakes were yet invented, but I pushed hard down on the brakes of that cart. I decided to buy for them more than I would have bought for myself. When I finished, I had spent all my money that I had saved.

On Easter morning, I rose very unhappily to go to the Easter Service. I just chose a dress that was not even for Easter or even close to a type of dress for Easter. It consisted of very heavy material. That Easter T.L. Lowery was having a baptismal service in a tent. When I arrived at the tent, I decided to sit in the very back, hoping that no one would see me. Thank God the Lord had other plans in mind! Our pastor and his wife had saved seats for us right down front. I have never been a shouting person, but I prayed that I would shout as Aunt Hazel once did.

The baptismal service seemed dead. Nevertheless, in an instant of time, the Holy Spirit began to move in our midst in a mighty way. All at once, I jumped up, ran down the aisle across the platform, and jumped into the baptismal pool shouting from one end to the other. The ushers could not pull me out of the pool. Our pastor said, "My God, if that water is holy enough to make Dot Roberts shout, let us all go into it." There were several hundred baptized that day. I was the first in and the last out. Guess what? That dress was holy; it went into the water with me and did not come up over my head. From this experience, I was reminded even to thank God for small blessings!

Our lives went along smoothly after that until we prayed for a son. Billy Jo Fain, a well-known evangelist, prophesied, in the sense of forthtelling, that Satan congregated over our house to destroy all of us the minute that my son was conceived in my womb. Do not the Scriptures say that Satan comes "to steal, and to kill, and to destroy" (John 10:10)?

In the tenth year of my marriage (without any children), the Lord led me to begin praying for a child. I remembered the people in the Bible who wanted children and how God moved and blessed them with a child. It seemed that the Lord began to put a seed of faith in my heart that led me to pray not only for a child but also for a son. After praying for some time, the Lord told me to name my boy, "Ricky Elias Roberts." When my husband came home from work that night, I told him that we would have a boy, and we were to name him, "Ricky Elias Roberts." My husband said, "No, we will not have a child!" The doctors had said that I must not have children due to medical reasons. I said, "We are going to have faith to believe that God can bring me through this, or we will hang up this thing called faith. We are either going to believe or reject our faith." As one can easily see, I meant business. I was determined to push forward to receive that which God had for me. Often we do not receive the things that God has for us because we will not push forward.

That night I conceived, and nine months later I had a boy. Even before that moment, all hell broke loose. The peace and rest that we had in our immediate family disappeared.

The pregnancy was not easy. I began to have all kinds of complications. The storms that would plague us began quite simply with two car wrecks in the seventh month of my pregnancy, and we were sued later.

Everything imaginable that could happen did happen in our lives. Satan literally came upon us like a flood. Satan truly is a coward. Why? To put it bluntly, Satan catches a person at his weakest times when a person has ended going through a battle between life and death. Then, Satan turns all his forces loose against that person.

However, in the midst of all these storms, God would use us to pray for people who were sick, and they would recover. All of these things especially happened after my son was born.

I experienced the Full Gospel of the Apostolic Church. I saw before my very eyes that God still performs miracles and healings; I truly saw that *Our God still liveth!* I saw the Words of Christ being fulfilled right before my eyes,

"They shall take up serpents; and if they drink any deadly thing, it shall not hurt them; they shall lay hands on the sick, and they shall recover" (Mark 16:18). I saw the words of James also coming to pass, "And the prayer of faith shall save the sick, and the Lord shall raise him up; and if he have committed sins, they shall be forgiven him" (James 5:15).

I remember going to St. Vincent's Hospital to pray for a little boy who was paralyzed. God healed him before I even went out of the room.

During this time, putting someone demon-possessed in my path or one who had gone into fanaticism was common for Satan to do. For instance, there was a woman who had been saved by the Lord only a few months and had gone into fanaticism, ahead of God, and began to walk around prophesying many crazy things.

All during this time while working, I was fasting up to twelve days at a time. Why? I was in need! I did not know how to handle this woman's situation and hysteria. Neither did I know how to handle the spirit of deception that fell upon this woman. This spirit of deception fell upon her so much that she thought she was the reincarnation of a famous prophet. Finally, she prophesied that if Elias and her husband would go to a certain place, they would find a man that would be able to help her. There was no such man because he just did not exist! This showed that the prophecies were not of God and that she had been deceived. She repented of her sins and became spiritually balanced by following 1 John 5:5-10.

All these experiences brought so much of a burden upon me that I backed off and stayed in my safety zone for some time. In other words, I would become lukewarm. In this lukewarm state, I found out that Satan would leave me alone. Why? I was no threat to him. Staying in the safety zone will not work. Just as the mother eagle will

29

push her babies out of the nest so any saint will have some battle to go through to gain what God has promised. As long as I remained in my safety zone, Satan was winning the battle for my son because I was no threat to him. Still, I want to tell everyone that when it came to my son and my family, I was ready and able to fight to the death (if need be) for them. Whatever I had to do, I was ready. I was ready to go into spiritual warfare. I was ready to go through dark places. I was ready to walk higher after God and His presence than I had ever walked before. Whatever I had to fight, whatever battle I had to go through, I was ready. I decided that no matter what I was going to oppose, I was going to hang on to the altar of God until I touched the hem of Jesus' garment. No matter what it took, I was going to touch that hem for my son. No matter what the cost, I was going to get to the hem of His garment. I was going to touch those nail-scarred hands because the Bible says, "By whose stripes ye were healed" (1 Peter 2:24). Praise God I intended to touch Christ Himself! I intended my son to be healed!

Thank God I had first hand experience with the retarded even before my son was born. My oldest sister, Myrtle, was born very severely retarded. I knew the heartache that surrounded our whole family and the helplessness that any family faces. Her retardation was due to a birth defect. The distress of my mother over her retarded daughter and the drunkenness of my father were so great that imagining how she survived is hard. The retardation of my poor sister was so great that the doctors told us that she would only live to the age of forty years. She lived to the age of forty-nine years.

When Ricky was born, the doctors said that I would never raise him because he was too sickly. I said, "Yes, but the Lord God gave him to Elias and me. We will raise him." During the first six years of my son's life, we slept with an alarm clock going off every thirty minutes. One minute, he would be all right; the next minute, Elias and I would be on our way to the emergency room with Ricky. We did not know that our child was mentally disabled or retarded. What does this mean? In his case, he had severe brain damage and dyslexia. We did not know that, even with his disability, Satan would turn even more against him and throw the fiery darts of sickness upon him.

In particular, Ricky would suffer terrible fevers and convulsions. It seemed that he suffered from sickness all the time. It seemed even that if he became excited or stressed out, his sickness would become worse. Since he could be sick at any moment, we could not even let him play like other kids. It seems that just a little change in our lives like weather or a little cold would bring on sickness. If he suffered fevers that were more than a hundred and one degrees, those convulsions would also be present. Ricky could change from being physically well to being physically ill within seconds. From moment to moment, Elias and I did not know what would happen. We did not know whether we would have a normal day or spend all day and night at the hospital. Often we found ourselves going to the hospital.

Satan even struck Ricky with a double set of teeth. These had to be surgically removed. Six or seven teeth had to be taken out at one time and braces added later.

Satan again struck against my son, not in any way that I could have ever imagined. One day Ricky woke up and could not walk. He was paralyzed. Our doctor knew nothing that could help; he could not tell us anything. We fell upon our knees and cried out to God. At the end of three months God, through His mercy, moved upon my son, and he was healed. He was able to take small steps and then larger ones. Finally, within days, all the effects that he had suffered from that attack were gone. He could normally walk.

As anyone can see, life literally became so hard that I cried many tears over my son and only wiped them away to begin anew.

It was in the midst of crying over my son that I called my son's pediatrician, Dr. Frame, and asked him if I could go to the office to talk to him about Ricky. I entered his office, crying hysterically, thinking that I was a bad mother since my son could not stay well. The doctor and I had a long talk, and he was very kind. He suggested that Elias and I put down carpet all over the house so that our son would not be on the cold tile floors. We did that, but it did not help. My son still had one cold after another, one sinus infection after another and suffered constantly with tonsillitis, bronchitis, ear inflammation and many other things. During the early years of my son's life if it was not one thing, it was another. This was clearly the truth for the fist six years of his life in particular.

These times were so bad that when we would rush Ricky to the hospital, the nurses already knew who we were. Since they knew who my son was, and they already knew what to do, they would usually meet us at the door in anticipation of what new crisis had befallen our family. All we knew to do was to stand and pray as Daniel did in Daniel 9. We did not have any idea of what in the world was happening to us nor what was going on to bring all these calamities upon our small but faithful family. All hope seemed lost; faith seemed to have reached its end in our lives. We had gone as far as we could physically go. When the breaking point comes in a person's life where faith may be lost and one is on his last leg, God will step into the picture someway and somehow.

Within the first six years of Ricky's life, God stepped into the picture in a particular and a special manner but

32

not as He Himself would do in the coming years. How did God step into the picture? He sent an evangelist to Jacksonville when my son was about four years old, and he prayed that Ricky would sleep because Ricky also suffered from insomnia. During these times of hellish sufferings in our family, my son hardly ever slept. When he did, he would only sleep for about 30 minutes at a time and then be awake for eight hours or more. The only time that Elias and I were able to sleep soundly and without worry during these times was when my mother-in-law would come down and take care of Ricky. My mother-in-law was a great praying saint of God who cried and prayed constantly for my son and for God to deliver him. However, she was not the only one to pray. Many, including ourselves, sought God's will for Ricky asking God to move beyond the realm of the possible into the realm of the impossible and to manifest a miracle for Ricky.

All these sufferings showed us that we could not do very much for Ricky. Whatever we did never seemed to help. This sense of helplessness brought us down to our knees. God was leading me into a season of intense intercession. To obey I had to be willing to eliminate everything that distracted me from perfect obedience.

I remember one day as I was cooking supper, Ricky had a convulsion and fell out of his high chair onto our tile floor. I did not move him until my neighbor came and checked to see if any bone had been broken. Another time, I was tied up in traffic and Ricky had a bad convulsion. All I could do was put my finger in his mouth to keep him from chewing his tongue and try to get him to a hospital. Elias and I never had any warning when he was going to have a convulsion. Yet, most of the time, God would never let me be alone when he had a convulsion. Thank God!

I remember the night he was going to graduate from kindergarten. That night Ricky had a double convulsion and his face turned black. I thought I was going to lose him! Thank God for the doctor and the nurse there that night! But they, as Elias and I, were truly helpless. They could only treat the symptoms. Thank God by prayer and laying hands upon my son, the Lord did heal him of convulsions that very night, and he never had another one.

As I look back, I realize the greatest decision Elias and I ever made was the night we became Christians. I had thought as a teenager that I needed Jesus, but I did not realize that I was going to need Him even more for my son. Elias and I began to realize that we had to have more help, and it had to come from God alone!

As Ricky continued to grow up physically, both Elias and I began to grow more serious about Jesus. Everything that the world had to offer meant nothing to us. All material things began to disappear and fade into the shadows of the intense sorrow over our son. For example, I loved coaching my softball team. Yet, I gave that up and began to study the Word of God and stay in my prayer closet for my son.

Elias and I began to realize that our son was truly retarded when he entered kindergarten. It did not take long to find out that he could not distinguish one letter from the other. When I found this out, I became more upset about him than I ever thought I would have to be. Both Elias and I became frantic that Ricky did not know the difference between letters. The kindergarten teacher tried to calm our concerns by pointing out that he was just a young five-year-old. In other words, he was not old enough and would begin to learn. I was to hear repeatedly, "Don't worry! He is just not old enough yet to learn." When Ricky began elementary school, the same statement was repeatedly said in both the first and second grades. The teachers gave excuse after excuse why Ricky could not learn. They accused him of suffering from excitability, anxiety, and hyperactivity. None of these accusations were true. They could not understand nor dare to concern themselves with the truth. They did not have time to worry about one child among countless children in the classrooms. They did not care about one child falling through the cracks of the school system.

Ricky's first-grade teacher, like all the others, said that he was just too young and would just have to repeat the first-grade.

No matter what my husband and I did to help Ricky learn, it was unsuccessful. Yet, we continued to try. For example, in and after the second, third, and fourth grades, we would put a card up on a wall before Ricky with letters written upon it trying to teach him the alphabet. This was also useless.

We would write on these cards clauses like, "Ricky and Snoopy [his dog]." As long as the cards were up, Ricky could repeat with us what was written on it. However, he could not pronounce any of these words nor remember the rest of the clause when the cards were taken down, hidden, or a part was covered. He would then begin to cry anew.

The next few years were no better. The school system and the teachers discovered no learning problem in Ricky. They passed him from grade to grade, and he could not even read a simple word.

One of my neighbors, Virginia Harrell, who was a substitute teacher, saw first hand how the teachers treated my child. They would not make him do anything. They would not even make him stand up for the pledge of allegiance. They gave up on him. But, thank God, we did not! But what is more important is that God never gave up on Ricky!

Ricky was just sitting in the classroom and taking up space. The teachers did not know what to do when I would go to talk to any of them. I even asked the school to have him tested. Yet, it did no good.

The absence of concern on the part of the school system made me almost ready to pull out my hair. The school system turned its back on my child and me. Because I was so concerned about my son, I made an appointment with the "School Guidance Clinic" through the School Board. The specialists kept Ricky for about three hours testing him. They called me with good news. Though he could not read a word or a letter, they said he was mentally normal, and all he had was a mother problem. They concluded that I was overprotective and that it was my fault. I was very upset that they received any of my tax money at all. Although speaking forcefully, I did not fall to their level. I acted as a Christian from the beginning to the end.

No matter what, I would not allow Ricky to be pushed or punished because he could not learn. All those supposed teachers and intellectuals desired that I punish my child because he could not learn. What kind of advice is that to a mother who has a retarded child? Remember what happened to Job in the Bible? All his friends and even his wife accused him of doing wrong, and so it was with me. Elias and I did have some faithful friends, but I had more of those types of "friends" that Job had.

While I am not a doctor or psychologist, I believe that the spirit of my son knew something was wrong with his brain. He knew that he was not like other children. Because Ricky realized this, he would sit and cry instead of having a happy childhood. To him, there was no such thing as a happy childhood or a life. I remember one time Elias and I caught Ricky paying kids to play games with him.

All the teachers and intellectuals did not see Ricky crying out from within himself. Thank God for the Holy Spirit that rose up in me to tell the educators that they did not know what in the world they were talking about! I would get help for my son one way or another! Since we still did not know what to do, we decided to hire tutors and place our son in a type of learning institution that dealt with children who have learning difficulties.

One of these institutions was known as the "Reading Researcher Institution," headed by Dr. Skinner. We still have the canceled checks proving that Ricky did enter this institution.

None of teachers and intellectuals did any good, and none could relieve the agony that our family suffered. It seemed that we had no hope. We lived in a state of hopelessness. Yet, in this state of hopelessness, we found ourselves even more on our knees crying out before God. We only found peace when we prayed.

Ricky attended another institution that has long ceased its operation. One day he ran out and busted against their glass door so hard that it is a wonder that the glass did not break. When this happened, Ricky came very close to having a nervous breakdown. Elias found Ricky shaking uncontrollably and trying to crawl underneath a car. Elias picked him up, wrapped his arms around him, and said, "Ricky, whether you ever learn, your mother and I love you. We will work and save for you." Ricky could never stand any person yelling at him to learn. The teachers of the institution yelled at all the students. How in the world drawing straight lines on a chalkboard teaches a retarded boy to learn to read, I will never know! When Ricky arrived home, I turned off dinner, took him in my arms, and said the same thing as Elias had said. We truly had a crying time!

Praise God I did not agree with any of their conclusions! Finally, I sought help through my son's pediatrician who had worked with us for so long in dealing with Ricky's problems. I told him my fears and my belief that Ricky suffered from a form of learning disability known as "dyslexia." He informed me that he believed that his son also had dyslexia. I asked him what he did. He said that he sent his son to a doctor who was the world-leading specialist in dyslexia. I said to him, "Would you please make an appointment for my son?" The doctor made an appointment for us to see this specialist.

Elias and I took our son to see him in Gainesville. Ricky was analyzed for three days. After this, the specialist called us in and told us that he was sorry, but there was no hope. Ricky not only had dyslexia but also severe brain damage that could not be cured medically. Ricky, according to this specialist, could never learn anything, would have to go through life three points higher than a moron, and had already come close to three nervous breakdowns in his young life. As he said this, the Holy Spirit rose up in me, and I said, "Oh! No! He won't! For as long as Jesus Christ sits at the right hand of the Father, my son will never go through life as that. I prayed for that boy, and God gives the best gifts."

The specialist stayed four hours with us and taught us how to raise him. Unknown to us, Ricky was outside the room listening to all of this. Have you ever tried to raise a child who knows that nothing can be done for him? The specialist told us whatever we did, not to spank him and never to allow other children to know his condition. Why? Other children would begin to harass him. This could make Ricky lose control of his anger and, with him having brain damage, he could hurt them or even worse he could become a killer. With all these terrible predictions, I stood up and proclaimed, "No! He will not do any of these things either!"

Leaving Gainesville and coming home was the loneliest time I think Elias and I ever spent. We had hit bottom. During the trip back home I sat very quietly with my arms around Ricky and spoke very few words, if any. When we finally arrived home, we made a new agreement with the Lord. It might be said that we made a covenant with the Lord. We gave the Lord everything we had. We cleaned out our bank account—the first time of three separate times in our lives—and gave God all that we had. We gave our son to God and dedicated him unto God since we could not raise him. In essence, we gave God our whole lives and began a new one with God. Both Elias and I began a life of fasting and prayer, seeking God to be over our child and over our lives.

It was in this fire of suffering our whole family faced that God purified us, especially Ricky, for his ministry, his calling, and his election.

Until that point in our lives, I can truthfully say that I had never been completely sold-out to God. I paid the preacher to read the Bible, understand its mysteries, and do the praying for the congregation and for the nation. Nevertheless, I am here to tell everyone that way of thinking does not work. God has called each of us to get into His Word.

Elias and I began to study the Word of God as God demands all of us to do. We began to research the Word of God, the church, its history, the history of theology, and why we believe what we believe. We began to teach Ricky about what the Bible says about faith, prayer, and healing. We would go to his bed at night, and I would read the Bible to Ricky and pray with him. I would tell him that God loved him and God wanted to heal him. I would quote the Scriptures on healing from Isaiah to James.

Unknown to us, we were not the only ones praying. After Elias and I would return to our room, we did not know that Ricky would cover his head up and pray that God would heal him and make him like other children. Ricky frequently prayed, "Lord, why can't I be healed and be like other children?" Often we would find his pillow wet with tears. For this reason, he had to admit finally that he also had been crying aloud unto God to be healed. It is a very heartbreaking thing to see your own son crying out to God with so much anguish and pain. He was retarded; yet, his spirit knew what was going on and how hurt he felt by children who would call him the "big fat moron."

Unknown to Ricky, he had entered into a life of prayer where patience is practiced, learned, and understood.

Ricky continued to pray, just like his father and I continued to pray. Our faith and our prayer life were all that we had. During these years, I especially prayed day and night, weeping before the Lord God for my son, lifting him up to the Lord, standing in the gap for him, and making up the hedge. I truly did not know what intercessory prayer was. I did not know half the time what I was doing!

In 1973, Ricky was still going to public school. The school system had continued to pass him from one grade to another. Finally, the school system had passed him into the sixth-grade even though he could not spell or write his name. At this time, Virginia Harrell again came to our rescue. She knew the public school Ricky attended was doing nothing for him. One evening she came to our house to tell us that University Christian School had a "Special Education Class" with only ten pupils in the class. She thought this would be a good place for Ricky since the teacher was trained to help disabled children.

The day that I took Ricky to sign him up for the class was a very bad day. Ricky was pitching a fit about leaving the public school for University Christian School. I would

40

drive a few miles and pull over, offering to carry Ricky back to the other school. I told him that he was going to go to school somewhere. At last, I pulled the car off the road, sat, and cried. He saw how bad this was affecting me and said, "Let's go on to University Christian School."

When Ricky was tested, the teachers found out that though he was twelve-years-old, he was mentally below kindergarten level. While it was utterly impossible for Ricky to enter "Special Education Class" at this time, God made an opening for him in that class somehow, and we took it!

He began going to this private school. This school helped all it could. However, there was very little that anyone could do for him. I still took him to tutors weekly. In the summer I began again trying to teach him at least one hundred words, and Elias and I continued to do everything that we could. Elias and I increased our prayers for him, and we had every preacher who believed in healing lay hands upon him and pray.

Going to this school helped relieve Ricky's frustration. He seemed to cry less. In fact, he was enjoying riding the bus. In a dream, the Lord showed Elias that Satan had set a trap for him at the bus stop. So, the school agreed to pick him up at our front door. That was a Godsend!

Throughout this time, Ricky was continually teased and laughed at by other children for his retardation. To this day, Ricky will only tell me some words he was called during these times. Dummy, stupid, moron, and retard are just a few. Now, Ricky continues to pray that those who called him such words as these will never suffer retardation. He would not wish this upon his worst enemies. He cries out for mercy and grace! Remember that Ricky had such low self-esteem that if he picked himself up, he would still be at the bottom. That is how low Ricky was!

University Christian School never left the "Special

Education Class" out of anything. For example, at Christmas the school had made a place in the Christmas program for all the kids, including those kids in the "Special Education Class." That night was so special for all parents to see their children having a good time. Ricky played the prophet Isaiah in this Christmas program, prophesying about the coming of the Messiah.

From 1973 to the fall of 1977, Ricky saw little success in learning. However, he did within this time limit move slowly from below kindergarten to that of the third-grade level. The short advancement was due to nothing but God working behind the scenes preparing for the greatest advancement in my son's life.

No further advancement or improvement could be seen for Ricky. As such, the battle for a miracle was continuing with very little fruit, if any. Elias, Ricky, and I continued to hold on! In all points Satan seemed to be winning, and we seemed to be losing until a night near Christmas that we will never forget. God gave us an early Christmas present beyond our wildest dreams.

4

AND THE OTHER STORMS SO RAGED

While Elias and I were having so many problems with Ricky, Satan struck against us from other directions with other storms. These storms complicated our lives as Satan and his forces sought our destruction. More than ever all these other storms were raging to prevent us from effectively battling for our son. Their purpose was to tie us down, weaken us, and turn our attention away from the miracle that awaited our son.

The first of these storms came through my sister, Myrtle, having surgery for intestinal cancer in Augusta, Georgia. The doctors did not expect her to live, and they called me to come and help. During this time, we had another bad car wreck and, at first my doctor would not allow me to go Augusta if I had to drive. Praise the Lord I had a friend who drove me up to Augusta in order to help my sister Ruby! I stayed a week. I felt like a yo-yo being pulled in many directions all at the same time. Ricky, my sister in the hospital, Elias, my job, and other things were all combined simultaneously to tear me apart.

When I went to Augusta and found the weakened condition of my sister, I cried. Not only had she had surgery with the doctors believing that she would not live, but the doctors also had put her through another surgery. Why? They had to remove a colostomy, which is the incision of an artificial opening into the colon for drainage.

The second surgery made things worse instead of better. She was hanging between death and life. My sister

Ruby and I had never seen anyone suffer as she did. She had such a high fever that she lay on a sheet of ice. She was frozen to that bed, and a thermometer was placed in her rectum always. Ruby would take the day shift; I would take the night shift. We also hired a private nurse around the clock to help us. However, Myrtle would know when we were in the room. If we were not in the room, her blood pressure would go through the rooftop. Though she was out of it and mentally disabled, her spirit knew. Ruby and I had to place a hand on her always.

One night she was so out of it because of her high fever that I sat on the bed with my hand on her until the early morning. She began to pray the most beautiful prayer of repentance that I have ever heard in my life. She spoke words that were not in her vocabulary. I knew that the Holy Spirit was guiding her spirit to pray this prayer. Yet, I knew that she was already saved in God's sight since she was retarded. God was allowing me to witness this awesome experience and giving me assurance that she was saved. Immediately, I remembered what Jesus had promised me a long time ago that He would save my family. This was another part of the promise that God had fulfilled. The tears began to flow down my cheek! I was not supposed to break down in that room, but I could not hold it any longer when I knew that God was honoring His Word to me. At that moment, the nurse walked in. I went into the bathroom to wash my face and to pray and cry anew. I told God that if she were suffering because of me, I had enough. What did He want me to do? The nurse knew that I had finally broken. I had to leave the room.

Ruby and I began bitterly to beg God to give her to us for another Christmas, and He did. Soon after Christmas Myrtle died, but I was at peace knowing that her spirit was in the hands of the Lord and that one day I would see her in Heaven, not as she was upon the earth but gloriously perfect.

The next person that Satan attacked was my mother. She had gone to see one of my sisters and that night a blood vessel in her stomach burst. My sister called for me to come and see if I could help her. I put Mother into the hospital with no insurance. This meant that Elias and I were held responsible for her bill. Praise the Lord I had a doctor that gave us a discount for both the hospital and his cost! Thank God we also could help her!

During this time, my mother-in-law also became seriously ill. She finally died years later from the continual storms over her health instigated by Satan.

I had been told that there is a bad seed in every family. If this is true, then my sister Sue was just that. I believe she was more like my father than the rest of his children. She was stubborn, prideful, rebellious, and demanded her own way. She was the type who loved the world and everything that the world could offer. This was her attitude and way of thinking until she went so low in depravity that even the world would not have her. She destroyed herself and her whole family. However, she was highly respected in her own community until sin found her and possessed her.

Sue loved the party life. She drank, danced, and committed all sorts of evil affairs. I do not think that I had ever seen a person as demon-possessed as she and her daughter became.

Sue thought that she could not give up the world and tried to find a type of Christianity that would fit her willful desire and satisfy her soul. She tried the Jehovah Witnesses and accepted the life of a Jehovah's Witness for a while only because the cult taught against the doctrine of hell. She finally began to see that there was a real hell, not just a hell upon this earth. How? This came about by no other means than her seeing for herself the reality of the supernatural. This reality of the supernatural was not in respect to God but to Satan. She allowed a witch to enter her home, live there, and saw first hand the power of Satan. This witch made many things move and hover throughout her home through spells and incantations.

I remember when her daughter was about three, Sue and her husband carried their daughter to a restaurant. The waiter asked the daughter, "What would you like?" The daughter replied, "A beer." Both she and her husband thought it was funny. However, it was not funny at all when their daughter grew up. The seeds of destruction were planted within their child, and she became extremely rebellious. She took countless kinds of drugs and drank many kinds of alcohol; she led a promiscuous and reckless life and caused several car wrecks. So much destruction was wrought upon Sue's whole family by all their lives that they lost everything that they had spent a lifetime making. Sue and her whole family had been blessed and bought everything they wanted, except happiness. By the time she accepted the Lord, it was too late for God to give her back what Satan had stolen.

One evening the Spirit of the Lord came upon me to pray for Sue and her family while they left my home going to their home. This was intercessory prayer, the same type as Paul mentions in Romans 8:26-27, "Likewise the Spirit also helps in our weaknesses. For we do not know what we should pray for as we ought, but the Spirit himself makes intercession for us with groanings which cannot be uttered. Now He who searches the hearts knows what is the mind of the Spirit, because he makes intercession for the saints according to the will of God."

In about two hours, I called their home and told them that God had shown me a wreck that I had been praying against for their survival. Immediately, Sue began to say that they had been in a bad wreck with a log truck and some people had been killed. No one could understand how Sue and her husband could have survived such a horrible wreck. However, I can. Can anyone see how important it is to follow the leading of the Holy Spirit? Satan had set a trap for them, but God was more than one step ahead of him. Even with God saving their lives, this did not faze my sister. She could have cared less about me praying for them and telling her about the wreck before she had a chance to tell me. She did not miss a heartbeat in her life of sin but continued to live that wicked life even more horribly than before this incident. Drugs, alcohol, and other vices were her gods. She made many sacrifices to her gods and received nothing but sorrow.

Standing by and seeing your family destroy themselves is very hard. So, I tried to get Sue help in various ways. Instead of thanking me for helping her and her family, she carried a loaded pistol around her home for about five weeks waiting for me to come in so that she could blow my brains out (as she termed it). Nonetheless, praise the Lord, He never allowed her to use it on me!

During this time, her husband even told a friend that if anyone discussed "that Jesus junk" in his store, he would demand that the person not come back. When a person walks beyond the critical point with God, then God turns him over to a reprobate mind and he is usually soon afterward destroyed (Romans 1-2). My brother-in-law was found dead soon after making that statement. How do I know this? Sue was at my house the day he was found dead. In fact, she was going to the hospital for the 15th surgery. She hated me so much that she said, "I would rather die and go to hell than to be in your home and have you help me." I saw the very hatred of Satan for me in her eyes. Satan said through her, "I hate your d...... guts." I said, "Yes, little sister I know, but I love you." When she said

47

this, I knew that God would separate us for my protection and the protection of my family. I began to cry in agony over this!

While in my home, the demons within her began to manifest themselves right before me as her voice and her face changed. What a hellish voice! I will never forget it! The hellish words that came out of her mouth were not her words but Satan's. I allowed my sister, in this shape, in my home around my husband Elias and son Ricky. Thank God the Lord told me that we all would be protected in the midst of so much hellish activity! I remembered that Satan, through his demons, wanted her to kill herself, and the Lord told this to me. I lay on the floor in front of her bedroom door where she could not leave to get a knife or another type of instrument to do herself harm. While she could not find any knife to cut her wrist, I did not know that she had sleeping pills with her. But, thanks be to God, He would only allow her to put the pills up to her mouth and that was all! She could not put the pills in her mouth; her hand and fingers would freeze when she tried.

After that horrible night, I arose to fix her a good breakfast. Then, I went to gas up the car. When I came back, she had the worst look on her face. I said to her, "What is wrong?" She said that her husband had been found dead. She and I were in shock. I carried her back to her home and then later to the Sheriff's office. When the Sheriff handed her all the possessions that were found on the body of her husband, I grabbed them and would not let her have them. I knew that these things would have the odor of death, and they had. Why? I knew that the body was found in a camper; it was very hot, and the body had been there for some time. I could not get the odor of death off my hands for several weeks. It was sickening!

Having to leave my home and stay in my sister's home

during her husband's death and funeral was an experience that I will never forget. There was no place, I believe, more demonic than her home. The demons of hell could literally be heard, yelling, howling, and screaming. I could hear the gnashing of teeth. The evil whispering that these evil spirits spoke so penetrated all the atmosphere of that home that I could only stay there by pleading the blood of Jesus over me. While my other sisters took a sleeping pill to fall asleep, I was vigilant. It was not a time to sleep but a time for battle! During this experience, I learned firsthand the power of the blood above every other weapon of our spiritual warfare.

During this time, the Lord came very close. He would show things to Elias and me that were going to happen to our family. One night the Lord showed me that my sister Sue would be shot at by noon the next day. Immediately, I began again, like all the other times of sorrow, to pray. But this time I prayed more powerfully than I have ever done. As I was praying, Satan spoke to me and said, "She will die tomorrow!" I told Satan, "No! As God liveth, She will not die!" I claimed her for the kingdom of God. I pled the blood of Jesus over her repeatedly.

The day Satan attempted to kill my sister was a very bad day. Shortly after noon, the extension telephone rang at work. A voice spoke over that telephone, "You have an emergency telephone call at the office." At that moment, the Devil really worked over my mind. Yes, he did! Sue had been shot at six times but was never hit. Praise the Mighty God whom I serve!

I decided that she was not going to hell. I was going to pray and fast until God moved somehow and saved her. Having no theology to discredit what God could do or what He had spoken to me, I believed in the promise God made to me. I held onto it with a death grip.

Sue suffered many problems, to say the least. She even

suffered physical ailments. One in particular was a spur growing on her spinal cord. The doctors did not discover this ailment until after her husband died. There is no pain like that pain. It made her more dependent on drugs and alcohol. The pain was so agonizing for her that the only relief she would ever have was when she was drunk or doped up. I just do not know how long she suffered with this. I am glad today that I had patience with her. Though still having this agonizing pain and remaining dependent upon drugs and alcohol, she did become better after her husband's death. She tried her best to keep the business going and deal with her daughter the best way she knew how.

Her daughter had not lived a rough life for a considerable time. She was a great wife to her first husband. She would have his breakfast fixed even if she had to get up at four o'clock in the morning. She had his clothes washed and ironed. What began her slippery fall was that this man she married left her when she had a child. From that point on, she fell deeper and deeper into the arms of Satan and his kind of life. She fell deeper and deeper into sin becoming more violent to all, including her own mother. One part of this kind of life was that Satan sent her another man who became her second husband. I believe this was the worst thing that could have happened to her. She became pregnant with his child, and the child in essence was born into a dysfunctional family. Again, she had a man who would not help her raise her child.

There were times that my niece was intoxicated or on drugs and she would try to kill her husband, her mother, me, or anyone else. She stabbed her second husband, and when he was recovering in the hospital, she pulled the tubes out of him. People literally became afraid of her.

With all of these problems, my sister never thought that she or her husband had any blame for how their daughter had turned out. I wish that my sister could have lived long enough to see her daughter's life change, and how she came a loving person, marrying a man that loved her.

One of the last times I talked to Sue and her daughter, Sue said, "I was not a good mother, but I am a wonderful grandmother." She no longer wanted to live that kind of life that sowed so many seeds of destruction. In the last years of her life, paralyzed and suffering from a stroke, she wanted Jesus. She called out to Jesus for mercy. The door of mercy had not yet shut. The Lord Himself heard her cries and in a vision came down to her. She saw Him in this vision-state walking one night into her room and telling her how long she had to live. That night she accepted the Lord. That night the hate, bitterness, and stubbornness melted away and what was left behind was a sweet and loving person who loved Jesus. What I saw God doing before my eyes took forty long years of fasting and praying to be accomplished. God kept His Word, but I did my part! In addition, from that night she continued to say often, "He's real! He's real. He's real." Jesus became the beginning, the middle, and the end of her speech. She ate, lived, and slept the Word of God. She was never the same again, and God continued to keep His Word about my family.

When Sue was finally put into a nursing home where I could go see about her without worrying whether I would have to fight her daughter, she only weighed sixty pounds. After working all day and driving about sixty miles to my job, I would run home, cook dinner, and drive about that far to carry her dinner. It took about two hours to feed her, one bite at a time. Soon after moving into the nursing home, she died and met the Master.

The next experience I remember in regard to my husband's family occurred one night in church where the Lord began to deal greatly with Elias about his baby brother. His baby brother, Wallace, was a deputy sheriff

51

in Coffee Country, Georgia. God showed Elias through a vision that his baby brother was going to be shot with his own gun. He told the preacher about what God had shown him and sought immediate prayer for his brother. The preacher anointed a handkerchief for my husband to carry with him to Georgia. When Elias and I arrived in Coffee Country, Georgia, to meet Wallace, he told us that as we were praying for him he was jumping down two stories of stairs away from a .38 pistol. We told him that this was not exactly what God had warned would take place. What God warned us about was that he would be shot within six months. We gave him the handkerchief and told him that since he did not have his mother any longer to pray for him, we were praying and would continue to pray.

One hour before the end of the sixth month, Wallace was shot with his own gun. At the same time, Elias was walking and crying out to God for mercy. When I came home from work that morning, Elias was looking out the window and saying, "God does not lie. Last night Wallace was shot in the chest. God spoke to me and said, 'Since you have given to Me both your life and your finances, I am giving back to you. Your brother will be all right.'"

When Elias went to the hospital, he was allowed to see his brother. Wallace told Elias that what the Lord had forewarned had happened. The bullet entered between the two main arteries of the heart. A hair difference and he would have been dead. What a miracle!

In two weeks time Wallace was in our home telling us about what had happened to him when he was shot. He said that he died and left his body. After leaving his body, he saw the ambulance that had been called. He knew who came into his house to help him. He rode with his body to the hospital. He saw the doctor and nurse run out to meet the ambulance, and he remembered what they said. But what is even more important is the fact that he saw the very hand of God come down from Heaven, hit his chest, and the nurse screaming out loud, "I have a pulse!" All the damage caused by the bullet was instantaneously healed. Instead of weeks of recuperation, he needed none. That is just like God!

I would like to say to the reader that his life changed because of that experience, but I would be lying. God gave him chance after chance, and he rebuffed them all. For the sake of Elias God spared Wallace, but instead of changing, he fell deeper and deeper into sin. Does not the Bible say that the wages of sin is death? Twenty years later, he committed suicide with the same kind of gun with which he was shot the first time and in the same place. What a tragedy!

Another turning event in my life and the lives of my family was the death of my sister Ruby. When I heard about her death, I began to cry bitter tears to God. I wondered why God took her because I needed her so badly. Ruby had always been the constant in our family, the one who would help and come to the aid of anyone. She had been of great assistance to our mother. Since I lived in Jacksonville and could only go up to Georgia occasionally, she was a Godsend. Ruby lived just across the branch from my mother and was taking care of her.

Before her death, one of the greatest events in her life was the Baptism of the Holy Spirit with the preliminary evidence of speaking in tongues. She had always wondered about speaking in tongues. She questioned whether they were biblical and whether they were for this day.

All came to a head one day when the Lord showed me in a vision that someone in our family would die. Of course, I began to cry out to God for help and mercy and began to speak in tongues before my sister as she and I were in the field picking butterbeans. She was shocked, awed, and worried. She had never seen anything as that.

She could say nothing, but "Baby, please get a hold of yourself! You are going to have a nervous breakdown!" I said, "Sis, can't you understand what this family is about to go through? We need to get a hold of God!"

When we came out of the field and I left her house, she fell upon her knees and cried out to God saying, "God if speaking in tongues is real, I want it!" Then, the power of the Holy Spirit overpowered her, and she began to speak words of a different language, unknown to herself. She had never expected anything like this—so much joy and peace unknown to her and unexplainable! In the midst of troubles, a person can have joy and peace by the Baptism of the Holy Spirit and the power that it releases. She never wanted to lose it. She received the Baptism of the Holy Spirit three years before she died.

When she had received the Baptism of the Holy Spirit, she and I would pray together in such completeness and in such power that both of us had never experienced before in our lives. Although I had the Baptism of the Holy Spirit years before she received it, I had not experienced this level of holiness and power. Why? According to Deuteronomy 32:30, two can put to flight at least ten thousand. This was the first time in our family that two Holy Spirit-filled saints were joined in the battle fighting against the forces of evil for our family, and we were winning the battle. There was another sister who was Spirit-filled, but she lived far away from the family and could not always join in the struggle.

While Ruby and I were winning the battle over our family against Satan, God warned me often, through speaking to me through dreams and visions, that Satan desired to kill my sister Ruby. I stayed on my knees and prayed using the passage about Hezekiah seeking God for mercy and protection (2 Kings 20:1). God moved and her life was extended for a considerable time.

Nonetheless, there are times when no one can stand up for you in spiritual warfare–you must fight alone. While my sister Ruby was Spirit-filled, she did not know or comprehend that she was in danger and needed to come against the wiles of Satan. She was under direct attack by witchcraft, and I warned her of this. But she would not listen. When God warns us and we will not listen, then the results can be terrible and disastrous. The results were truly terrible and disastrous. I believe that she succumbed to the plans of Satan and died. She died before her time and under the permissive will of God. For if God had not allowed this, it would not have been done. It was her choice and her will. The only thing that God did was to allow it. But it was not His original intention.

My son explains the fulfillment of God's Word and His intention in connection to free-will in this way:

> The fulfillment of God's Word and God's intention is not placed outside the sphere of human freedom and choice, and most often is dependent upon free moral agents to become fulfilled. It is grace that demands that the intentions of God must allow free moral agents a choice to accept or reject God's will for their lives. When God uses a choice done by free-will agents, He works to turn the actions of men and other creatures into a method or means by which His plans may be fulfilled. In other words, He takes those actions that are contrary to His will and takes hold of the consequences and changes things so that they may be beneficial to the fulfillment of His plans.

The day I heard from a telephone call that my sister Ruby had died, I lost it. I went into shock; I could not believe that God would do this to me. I cried out loudly and bitterly walking throughout the house, yelling, "God,

55

what are You doing to me? Do You love me? Didn't You know that the family needed her? Why have You forsaken me?" I needed her so badly to help me go through the family troubles and to give me courage. We were such a comfort to each other and a shoulder upon which to cry. She was the very heart of the family. That night I walked in the backyard (for some time) saying, "God, Why?" Repeatedly, all night, I asked the same thing. I asked, "Don't You love me? What have I done that I have had to go through this alone?" It seemed that God was a thousand miles away or that God had turned His face from me. What an awful feeling to feel that God has forsaken you! My life, which was already shaken, became worse and the storms of life were truly raging.

Elias did not say anything about the death of Ruby until we were on our way to the funeral. I could not say anything except, "Why God, why?" Elias was the one that God enlightened and gave the reasons for her death. Elias simply said that God did not tell me about her death because I would have prayed and fasted until He would have spared her again. It was not my time to do all this, but it was the time for Ruby to step up and heed the warnings of the Lord. In addition, he said that my mother was another reason that God allowed this. Why? As one will easily see, God allowed my sister Ruby to die at this time so that the God of the miraculous could completely save my mother.

In the midst of Ruby's funeral, I was wondering what my family and I were going to do about Mother. Mother had burned herself very badly three days before the death of Ruby. I had seen this in a vision days before it happened as a warning that was not heeded. I told Ruby that Mother was unable to live by herself due to her age and health.

The day of Ruby's funeral my family and I had to put

Mother in the hospital to put a skin graft on her arm. This was a terrible time. Not only had my sister Ruby died and my mother had burned herself, but also one of my sisters and a cousin had found my mother sitting on the floor throwing up until she finally passed out. This took place after she came home from the hospital. The doctors had not yet found out the cause for this.

I brought my mother home with me and put her under my doctor's care. When he checked her over, he found that she had cancer of the liver and would start to throw it up very soon. I said, "No! She will not!" I went to my car and began to cry out to God saying, "Lord, You promised me that You will not let more be put on me than I could bear" (1 Corinthians 10:13). Immediately, the Lord spoke to me, "Go on a five day fast." I did, and it was not long before a few of the nurses began to fast and pray with me. Three days after completing the five-day fast, the doctor came in her room and said that he wanted to send her to another hospital for a C.A.T. scan. At that time not all hospitals had this equipment. From Thursday through Saturday morning, the hospital ran tests and more tests. Finally, the doctor came into the room a little disturbed and bewildered. He simply said, "I do not know what to tell you about your mother. Other doctors and I have consulted together about the diagnosis and have come to the conclusion that your mother had liver cancer, but now her liver is as normal as yours and mine. I don't know what happened." I said, "Doctor, do you believe in fasting and praying?" He said, "Yes!" I said, "Doctor, God had put me on a fast!" He said, "Take her home!"

This was the beginning of nine years of what can only be called "hell." It was hell because I was still dealing with a son who was retarded and a mother who was truly demon-possessed. Please understand that my mother was the hardest person to take care of that anyone has ever seen. This was a time of the greatest intercessory prayers that I have ever prayed.

After my sister Ruby's death, in a vision, the Lord carried me away into hell. I fell down deeper and deeper into a deep pit. This falling lasted for a considerable time. When I arrived in hell, there was darkness everywhere; yet, there was a light in the midst of that darkness. That light must have been the light of God shining even in the midst of hell itself. It must have been the Shechinah Glory--the divine presence of the Lord, which was manifested. This light penetrated far enough to see what was going on. Though I did not literally see the dead, I saw the appearances or forms of many in hell. I saw the forms of some that I knew did not live a holy life and were already dead. God was telling me that they had gone to hell. I saw the forms of people who were still living. I knew God was telling me that they were destined for hell if they did not change. One of these was my mother. I saw her form hanging and looking over hell. This meant that she would go to hell if she did not change. When I saw her form, I cried out to God, "Don't let her go to hell! Her life has been so hard!"

After leaving the vision-state, I ran into the living room and told my husband what had happened. He said, "Your mother is not saved." The whole purpose of the vision was a warning that my mother was not saved. She had gone to church for many years and was not saved. She had lived as a hypocrite for years. She knew about Jesus, but she never met Him. How do you get someone to realize that he or she is unsaved so that he or she can be saved?

About three weeks later, a tent revival came to Jacksonville. All of us, including my mother, went. The preacher, who I had never seen before, said to me, "I am going to eat breakfast with you in the morning." He later told Elias that my mother had to repent of her sins and especially of sins that she believed God would never forgive. He came to our home and talked to her personally and privately. She believed that God would never save her because she made herself have two miscarriages. Before birth control was available, it was common for a woman to make herself have an abortion.

While she was not saved, at this point, the beginning of her deliverance began. As in the early church, some will be delivered from demon-possession only in stages; here is a clear example of this. Until one is completely delivered from demon-possession, the early church said that a person could not be saved.

I wish I could say that the preacher's talk to her was all it took for her to have peace and be saved, but Satan did not want to give her up. It was a battle of hellish proportions. Elias and I had to live in intercessory prayer; we had to learn even more deeply the profession of intercessory prayer. It is, in its own right, a ministry and a way of life that will touch God when nothing else can touch Him. It will open doors that nothing else can open; it will bring down strongholds when nothing else can break them; it will win the battle of spiritual warfare over our lives when nothing else can even win. In essence, intercessory prayer, equipped with the Baptism of the Holy Spirit and the evidence of speaking in tongues, will empower the saint of God like nothing else.

Intercessory prayer and tears are interlocked. Tears touch God when nothing else can. Why? They are linked to intercessory prayer. Then, intercessory prayer and tears both touch God when nothing else can. Tears are part of intercessory prayer.

Elias, Ricky, and I finally found out what was troubling Mother. First, we saw three demons come out of her, each looking like black cats. Second, one night we heard a horrible scream come from her room. My son and I ran in her room and she was saying very loudly, "Get those babies off me and my bed!"

What had happened in her life? Since my sister Myrtle was retarded, could not walk early in her life, and everything that she ate had to be cooked for three hours, Mother was afraid of having other retarded children. So, she made herself have two miscarriages. For all these years, she had carried the guilt of those horrible acts. These acts made her have nervous problems and led to several nervous breakdowns and her having to enter a mental hospital. As such, she had to be under a doctor's care for years. Does anyone have any idea how Satan tormented her and made her think that God would not forgive her for what she had done? What a burden she had to carry all those years!

It was very common during the time that I was taking care of my mother for me to beg God to let a transfer truck hit me head-on so that I would not have to keep going on with all the problems that we were facing. I was reaching my greatest point of despair and fatigue. Even some people in the Bible, on occasions, wished to die. Remember Jonah and what he said, "And it came to pass when the sun did arise, that God prepared a vehement east wind; and the sun beat upon the head of Jonah, that he fainted, and wished in himself to die, and said, 'It is better for me to die than to live'" (Jonah 4:8).

During these years of hell, Mother always wanted to be right under my feet. Even while she was in the hospital, I had to stay with her. She tried to dominate my life and the lives of Elias and Ricky.

One cold day in January my mother had been acting nervous, walking the floor and becoming mentally unstable. She came to my bedroom at eight in the morning. The woman who had helped us with Mother for five of the nine years arrived at our home at 8:15 a.m. Between

8:00 a.m. and 8:15 a.m., my mother left the house, entered the backyard, walked to the creek, jumped in, came back to the house, and was at our door waiting for this woman to come. When the woman came, my mother, wet and muddy, walked behind her. My mother admitted that she had tried to commit suicide by jumping into the creek behind our house. She said that every time she would put her head under the water, an angel of God would physically jerk her head back up. She tried to kill herself several times and every time the angel of God would prevent it. That the angel of God did this can be seen. My mother was quite old and unable to climb up and over the bulkhead that was placed between the creek and our backyard. Doing that would have been impossible for her apart from divine assistance.

What could I do? I put her into the bathtub with warm water and washed her. Then, I walked down behind the house to see what I could see. I saw where she had come out. I saw that the rocks and the cement that the bulkhead was made of were still wet and muddy. How could I have ever gotten over her drowning? How messed up and how sickly she had to be to do this to herself! I called the doctor and carried her to the hospital. The doctor found out that medication caused her to become very unstable mentally.

Frequently, my mother in those years would be rushed to the hospital, especially for heart failure. She had been at death's door more times than can be counted. Doctors repeatedly would think that she would not make it out of the hospital. Yet, she always did.

One time when she became very sick, we carried her to the hospital and for three days I took care of her every minute. I did this so much that I did not have any time for a cup of coffee or to sleep. During these three days, her bowels continued to run off and she continued to cough. My mother became so sick that I was forced to hold her on the bed and keep the I.V. in her arm.

At the end of the third day, the doctor came into my mother's room and told me he could not find what was wrong with her. He could not help her. Whatever was wrong or whatever type of sickness she had, it was killing her, and he could not find it. Repeatedly, throughout much of my life, I cried out to God. The Lord told me it was a bird fever and gave me the name for it. I told the doctor what the Lord had said. The doctor looked at me very strangely, and then he turned around and ran out. About one hour later he came back into the room and said that he did not have time to check out that she had bird fever, but she had all the symptoms. He said she was dying and he did not have time to test for this fever. I said, "Go ahead and treat her for that! I will take the responsibility!" He had to quarantine us. The Lord finally delivered my mother from the bird fever a few days later. I was exhausted after this stage of the battle, but the battle for my mother was still not over.

Of course, Satan knew that I could go no further, and he had my sister Sue call the hospital and curse me for everything in the book. Finally, I knew that I could go no further. So again I began to cry out to God, "What is wrong that I have to go through this by myself? Lord, I can't go another night without sleep!" The Lord spoke and said, "You have not because you ask not!" It did not take me long to ask Him for help, and in about ten minutes, the telephone rang and a friend called to see if I needed help.

Mother got to where she would suffer insomnia until about five o'clock in the morning. During this time, she would be calling out all night long. Elias and I began to pray about that. We would go into her room and cry out before God for her night after night. Nevertheless, it seemed that we could not get through with one thing until another took place. What I have said here are just some things that we had to go through with her.

All of these storms were going on while Elias and I were crying out to God for our son to be healed, and we were also going anywhere that a revival was taking place in order for my son to be prayed for by godly men or women who had the gifts working through them. I wanted someone to touch God for our son. When you need something from God bad enough, money and every other thing do not matter and neither does denomination.

The storms of problems, Satan instigated within the families of both Elias and me, became so horrible in our lives that they literally began to destroy all hope for our son to be healed. As one can remember, their purpose was to tie Elias and me down, to weaken us, and to turn our attention away from the miracle that awaited our son. These storms were turning Elias and me away from our son and away from others to be prayed for and upheld to the Lord. These storms were causing so much destruction that God commanded that their interference be brought to an end. The storms of problems were interfering with my journey to touch God's heart for my son.

But how and when did God command this? God did not focus his rebuke and command upon my husband but upon me. God saw that I was the anchor for my son's healing, and He demanded that the anchor change so that Elias would change his direction of prayer.

This all came to a head one night when the Lord spoke to me while I was in the lab at my work and said, "Put thy family on the altar and leave them there!" I was not ready to let my family go to hell. I meant I was going to hang on to that altar. I was going to press through to God. I was going to plead with God. I was going to argue with God until He moved. But when He told me to put my family on the altar and leave them there, I showed God a Scripture in the Bible where it said that the one that kept knocking received (Matthew 7:7-8). I said, "Now, Father, I do not want to be disobedient unto You or do anything wrong, but according to this Scripture, the one that keeps knocking will receive, and if You can confirm this in another way, I will do the best I can to lay them on the altar and leave them there." Do not ever say that to God unless you are ready for something to happen!

Approximately a week after that, I went to hear a minister, W.V. Grant Sr., who came into Jacksonville to preach on the Battle of Armageddon. In the meantime, I was also doing much research in the Bible, especially about the Battle of Armageddon, the Second Coming, the Rapture, and other future events.

So, I wanted to hear this man and what he had to say. I went over to the church that night and there were nearly two hundred people outside the church who could not even get in. All at once, a man took me by the elbow led me through the crowd into the church. He sat me down in the second row right on the aisle. I looked around the church to see if any older people were standing up by the wall to hear this man preach and teach the Word of God. Any other time I would have risen up, given my seat to someone else, and would have gladly stood up by the wall. However, this time something stronger than I prevented me from doing this. When the minister came forth to the platform, he said, "Well, Sir, I said I was going to preach on the Battle of Armageddon if the Lord let me! Yet, God changed my text when I came into this church! It is for this young lady sitting right here! I am going to teach you how to pray tonight! God has called you to be an intercessor! He called you to pray for other people! He loves someone else besides you and your bunch! He wants you to put your family on the altar and leave them there!"

God had answered what I had asked Him to do, to confirm it, and He did. Have you ever laid someone on the altar when Satan was trying to kill him or her? Have you ever had to sit back and watch God work instead of you getting involved? When this happens, all Satan is going to do is loose every one of his imps against you and your family to try to destroy all of you. Your trials and tribulations with these people are going to increase. It was so hard when a relative would call me and say that she had tried to commit suicide and was in the hospital, and I could not run over there. It was so hard when the same relative would call and say that she did not have any money to buy anything. Having tough love is hard. Nevertheless, you wonder how you are going to do that when you have Jesus' love. You do not want anyone to mock your Christianity. You want to walk as Christ walked. I did not quite understand what the Lord meant at first about laying them on the altar and leaving them there. I remember many days and nights when I would have to hang up the telephone. When the telephone would ring, I would tremble all over. I did not know what to do and neither did I know what was happening. There was one thing after another for so long. So much horror was taking place in our lives that when the telephone would ring, I would just begin trembling. Then, I would hang the telephone up, go back, lie on the bed, and weep violently.

I finally understood that by placing my family upon the altar, I was surrendering them into God's hands and turning my attention firmly toward praying for my son first and then others.

These are just some of the storms we had to endure. Always one problem would begin before another problem ended. There was never a time that could be considered a time of peace.

All these times I would pray and be led into fasts from

three to twenty-one days in order to break through the barriers of the demonic. Praying and fasting helped! Apart from both praying and fasting, we may not have survived to tell the history of our lives and about what God has so wrought.

5

RECEIVING THE PROMISE

In 1975, I experienced something beyond expectation and something that words can hardly describe. It was a very humbling and very strange occurrence. I was in the extra room, within our home, that had become the prayer room on my knees praying. Nothing was unusual until the Spirit of God rushed into the room and overshadowed me. Then, the Holy Spirit gave me a vision. In this vision, I saw one of the same wheels that Ezekiel had seen in Ezekiel 1 and 10. This wheel came rolling into my room in the early morning. This wheel, which is in actuality a type of angel, came to do God's business and may be known as a wheel-angel. This wheel-angel broke through the demonic layers that had tried to bind and imprison us. He came to deliver a message of hope and to bring a promise.

His appearance can best be described as a wheel in the midst of a wheel. This means that this angel had the appearance of an inner and outer wheel jointed to make one individual wheel. The wheel-angel that I saw had four sides and did not have to turn to go in the direction that he wanted to go. His color was that of amber or beryl. This is understood to mean that the color of the wheel-angel, in this instance, was that of golden-yellow, not a green. The rings of the wheel were full of eyes. The wheel-angel had the ability to speak, and his voice was as the voice of many waters all sounding in sequence. The glory of God that surrounded him lit up the room. While I had seen angels before this event, I had never seen such as this. I have never forgotten it, nor can I. The whole miracle of my son's healing is founded upon this vision; it became the lifeline. In essence, all things that God gave to us afterward were used to confirm this vision.

In the midst of this vision, I saw a large wheat field and a sickle going about by itself (without anyone using it) cutting down the wheat. In the midst of the vision, I saw large storehouses that were being filled to the brim. The wheel-angel spoke to me and said, "The wheat field is the world of sinners; the sickle going about cutting down the wheat is the 'End-Time Harvest'; the storehouses are the churches, which are alive not dead and give the Holy Spirit a place in their services. These storehouses will be filled to the brim." In other words, the Lord, through His angel, promised another Great Awakening in the end times, which would take place before the Rapture of the Church.

The wheel-angel also showed me a man and said, "This is for you."

Since I was not a biblical scholar, I did not know what the "wheel" was there for when I saw it. I did not know that it was a very powerful angel or that Ezekiel had seen four of these wheels himself more than 2,500 years ago. I was alone, not knowing whether I was crazy or moving into a realm of fanaticism. I was truly upset. The church that I had attended (though believing in the spiritual gifts of the Holy Spirit, visions, dreams, and other manifestations of the Holy Spirit) had not been taken as deep as I was going.

Praise the Lord I prayed for help! God led me to call my sister-in-law, Evlen Roberts Cox. She was and still is a Church of God minister. I told her what had happened. She informed me that what I had seen is found in the

Bible. I had explained the wheel exactly as Ezekiel had seen him. Yet, I told my sister-in-law, "This vision cannot be of God. The angel showed me a man, saying, 'This man is for you,' and I have a husband already." She told me that this was not what the wheel-angel meant. She said, "Hold on to the Lord, let nothing divert you from the goal set before you by God. Whatever was going on was truly God, hang on." She also said to wait and allow God to unravel the mystery about the man. So, I waited. Within three weeks, what the wheel-angel had spoken about a man did come to pass, but not before Satan tried to kill me three separate times.

One day while I was going to work, a bad thunder and lighting storm came out of nowhere. In fact, I have never seen lighting as bad as it was that day. The lighting was striking and running down the road ahead of me. Suddenly in a vision-state, I saw Satan himself enter my car. He said, "I am going to kill you before you arrive at work." I rebuked Satan, and said, "You are a liar and have been from the beginning of your sinful career! You know that you cannot touch me much less kill me if the Father does not let you! I have been bought with the blood of Jesus!" The lightning was striking up and down the highway as I was speaking to Satan. I kept driving and Satan kept talking to me until I arrived at work. When I arrived at work, three men were standing under a shelter waiting for the storm to pass. As I got out of my car with an umbrella over my head, lighting struck over my head. The three men were screaming because the lightning was striking so close over my head, they thought that I had been hit. I kept on walking. A small voice on my right side spoke in my ear, "You better hurry up! Satan is going to get you!" Another voice on my left side said, "Let not fear enter therein!" I deliberately walked very slowly. That night my arm did feel little twinges of pain, but that was all.

At the last point of this three-week period, on a Sunday, I felt like I was going to have a nervous break down. I could not be still! It was as if I had fire shut up in my bones. Truly I was experiencing, unknown to me, what Jeremiah underwent. Does not Jeremiah say, "His Word was in mine heart as a burning fire shut up in my bones and I was weary with forbearing, and I could not stay" (Jeremiah 20:9)?

I would try to read a Christian book and the more I read, the more I would burn, and the more I would be nervous. It was so bad that Elias told me to go to the hospital so the doctors and nurses could find out what was going on. Naturally, neither the doctors nor the nurses could find anything wrong with me. They sent me home.

On the way home, I turned on the radio and a program was advertising that a tent revival was taking place that night on Old Kings Road in Jacksonville. As I was listening to the radio, the Lord told me to go to that revival. I told my husband that night about this revival and that I was going. He did not want me to go that very night because I was sick.

Regardless, I went to the tent revival. Standing on the platform was the man whom I had seen in the vision three weeks earlier. When he took the microphone, he said, "My meeting here in Jacksonville is over." I said to myself, "I have just gotten here." Then, the evangelist said, "A prophet is coming into Jacksonville and will use my tent to hold a revival. If this man tells you that you are going to die, you better make your funeral arrangement!" The evangelist continued and stated that this prophet, who was Billy Jo Fain, was once a bank robber and on the F.B.I. top ten list. He went on to state that this man was tried and sentenced to a ninety-nine-year prison sentence. Yet, his praying mother cried out to God, reminding God that even before his birth her son had been called to be a prophet, and the life he was living was not what was promised. God set this man free from a ninety-nine-year sentence. He became a minister for God.

When it came time for the evangelist to pray for the people, he called me up out of the audience and told me to lay hands upon the people. Later, he told me that he saw from the pulpit that I was engulfed in a flame of fire and needed to pray for the people. I found out that praying for people was the only means for the anointing of God to be released from me and its power to be diminished within my bones. It was the anointing of God that was flowing from God to me and needing an outlet. I had never been taught that the anointing needs an outlet. The outlet comes only by praying for people and especially laying hands upon others. When I prayed for others, the burning lessened and stopped only temporarily. It would come back as God willed for me to pray for others.

When I came home and told Elias and Ricky what had happened, Elias said immediately, "There will be false prophets before the end time deceiving many! We must guard ourselves against all deception! We will not go!" I spoke to him very calmly and said, "You may not go, but the Lord is dealing with me. I am going!" When it comes right down to it, we all must obey God rather than men. Remember what Peter and the other Apostles said, "We ought to obey God rather than men" (Acts 5:29). All must understand that Elias did not see the vision. He did not have the power of the Holy Spirit moving him to go to the tent revival. He was worried about me going off the deep end and about me following false prophets and false teachers. We finally agreed to lay out a fleece before God as the saints in the Old Testament times had done when they did not exactly know the will of God for themselves or for their nation (Deuteronomy 18:4; Judges 6:37; 6:38; 6:39; 6:40; Job 31:20). We prayed that if this prophet was from

71

God, he would call all three of us out at once and pray for us. I had never seen that happen before. We felt that it would be a very good test to determine whether he was of God or not.

On a Wednesday morning, Billy Jo Fain had his first service in that old tent. I drove a separate vehicle from Elias. Elias and Ricky went together in another car. All three of us sat in different locations within the tent. We were trying the spirits as John warned all saints must do (1 John 4:1-3).

When this prophet came up on the platform to preach, he looked at my son and said (I will never forget it), "Young man, you have a learning disability. Can I pray for you?" He then pointed to Elias and said, "This is your son! Come up here!" Next, he turned to his left and pointed to me saying, "Come up here! All three of you are a family!" He told us to join hands. Then, he told us about our life and how Satan had congregated over our home from the minute Ricky was conceived although this prophet had never seen any of us before this time. He described all that had been happening to us, repeated that we had been in eight wrecks, and even described the time clock going off every thirty minutes for the first six years of Ricky's life.

He continued to lay out several other words from the Lord about Ricky, about us, and about what God intended for him: 1) Ricky is ordained of God; 2) He is consecrated and dedicated unto God; 3) He is terribly retarded with no hope, except from the Lord; 4) He will never be of the world but in it only; 5) The Lord will heal him very shortly for an End-Time Harvest; 6) God Himself will educate Ricky; 7) God had brought us out of our church because He did not want Ricky to be contaminated by tradition; 8) God will not allow man and their traditions to teach Ricky; 9) God will allow Ricky to go to college, but Ricky will teach the college; 10) Ricky would learn the Bible from the ancient languages and from the ancient church; 11) Ricky will turn the church world upside down.

I am glad that a preacher never taught me erroneously about the prophetic word. I am very glad that I never heard that prophecy is only universal and can only be given to a whole nation, a whole congregation, and not to an individual. What good is the prophetic word for edification when it is only said to be universal? What does the saint do when he is crying out for God to give him some direction? What about all the times in the Bible when the prophetic words were not given to a nation but to a person. Remember Ahab, David, Paul, and a host of others (1 Kings 21:11-22:53;Jeremiah 11:21; 14:14; Ezekiel 29:2; 37:2; 38:2; 1 Samuel 9:1-27; 2 Chronicles 15:3; Nehemiah 6:12; Proverbs 30:1; 31:1; 2 Chronicles 18:7; 20:37; John 11:51; Isaiah 7:14; Jude 14; 1 Kings 1; 11:29-43; 13:18-20; 14:2; 16:7; Acts 21:1-13; 2 Samuel 7:8-17; 12:1-8).

It was this prophet, Billy Jo Fain, who gave a prophetic word about an End-Time Harvest beginning here in Jacksonville and spreading all over the world. This word confirmed the vision.

It was this man that prophesied that counterfeit revivals would spring forth mightily before the End-Time Harvest and that genuine forerunner revivals would also spring forth as indications that the great revival is at hand. I have seen Billy Jo Fain's words come to pass. There are many counterfeit revivals going on now, and there are several genuine Holy Ghost burning revivals going on. However, none of these are that great revival in which our family will have a part. God healed a retarded teenager for this great revival.

It was this man that gave prophetic words directed for this family. It was this prophet who spoke mighty words about this family's part in the End-Time Harvest and about this family's ministry being based in Jacksonville. Other prophetic words he spoke will not be mentioned because they have not yet been fulfilled.

After receiving several prophetic words that morning, late that night my husband cried out to God and asked God, "Why? Why? Why? Why were we chosen to receive the promise and the blessings?" The next morning of the revival, the prophet called him out and retold exactly what he had said. The prophet said, "It is not you. It is God's sovereignty and especially His grace!"

I had the vision of the angel a little more than three weeks before this experience. This man was the first prophet that I had seen and the first prophetic word from a prophet that I had ever heard. Since prophecy was new to me, I could do nothing but believe. I had nothing else to hold onto except the prophecy and the vision. This prophecy confirmed the vision. Both these things were like a stick in the midst of a mighty river onto which a drowning victim could hold. I did just that. I held onto the vision and the prophecy united as one small stick, yet mighty. It saved me from drowning in a river of hopelessness.

It took an exalted faith to prophesy over us about all these things. I am very glad that Billy Jo Fain lived long enough to see God heal and educate Ricky.

It was during these times that this great tent revival gave birth to other revivals in Jacksonville and Fernandina, which are still having effects today. This great tent revival is where Ricky experienced the "Baptism of the Holy Spirit" and where my son first heard the voice of God audibly. The prophet told him that God desires to speak to him like a friend talks to another person, face to face. After hearing that Ricky went home, went to bed, and waited. Finally, God broke through the demonic barrier trying to prevent God speaking to my son. Ricky, for twenty-four hours, heard the audible voice of God. His room was filled with the Shechinah Glory–the divine presence of the Lord manifested–so much that the smoke filled the room visibly. Many things were spoken to him that night, some things unknown to everyone, except the Lord and Ricky. This was not the last time that Ricky was granted the privilege of hearing the audible voice of God for twenty-four hours.

After that experience, Ricky was given his first vision experience. He saw Heaven open, and the hands of God coming down and breaking through the dark clouds. Underneath the hands the words were written, "For I shall bring forth truth out of darkness for the sake of my people." The Lord said, "This will be your logo for the ministry."

It was during this revival that several mighty manifestations of the Lord took place.

The first manifestation was a blue mist. It invaded the tent visibly; it went around the tent and touched my sister Sue three separate times. As the mist passed over the heads of the people, many fell out as if they were dead. It was a mighty sign of God's providence.

The second manifestation was what happened to a co-worker of mine when she came to the revival. Though she had never gone to a Pentecostal revival, she would never forget this one. She accepted the Lord as her Savior and she experienced one of the most severe cases of being drunk in the Spirit that I have ever seen in my life. She stayed drunk in the Spirit for five straight days. At work, I saw her myself stagger from one side of the hall to the other saying, "Be not drunk with wine but with the Spirit saith the Lord!" Needless to say, I was begging God to lift the Spirit from her. So many people from all over the mill were coming to see what was going on. On Wednesday my boss came in and said, "Dot, whatever you threw on her, get it off! She is going to blow us all up!" I said back, "I have thrown nothing on her, and if this is of God, we will all be all right! But if not, we will be blown up!" With all this going on there was much repentance and silence at the mill!

The third manifestation was a visible manifestation of an angel. One night a man appeared in front of the tent. This man was truly strange. He spoke with such wisdom and had such a holy appearance that there was no question that this man was an angel. His appearance was absolutely beautiful: blue eyes, blond hair, and other such features. Why did he come? I had been studying about demons and was not yet mature enough to handle the topic of demons. For when a saint studies demons, these evil spirits will congregate around the saint. Therefore, the saint had better know how to fight them. The first thing I said to him was, "I am studying demons." He said, "Why study on demons? Study angels! They help the saints." I was dumbfounded. I thought studying on demons was something big. The angel of the Lord said that it was nothing. I learned much from our conversation. The last thing I said, "Can we pray for you?" He said, "Yes!" In humility, he bowed his head and accepted our prayer. How do I know that this was an angel? Since then, this same man has appeared in two visions proclaiming himself as an angel of the Lord and coming in the name of the Lord. From our conversation, I found out that he believed and still does that Jesus Christ was born from a virgin, was crucified, and arose from the grave. He also proclaimed that Jesus Christ is God. In other words, he accepted all the fundamental doctrines of Christianity. Remember Hebrews 13:2.

It was during this same revival that Elias had two notable experiences from the Lord. The first can only be described as amazing. It was not a vision nor a dream but what is known as a "translation" or "a rapture." In an experience as this, a person is either caught up bodily as with Enoch, Elijah, and Philip (Genesis 5:24; 2 Kings 2:9-12, and Acts 8:39), or his soul is caught up without the body.

In the case of Elias, his soul was caught up, not to Heaven but to the valley near the mountain where the body of Moses was buried. There Elias appeared within this valley. As he turned and looked, numerous people were sitting down in countless ranks doing nothing at all. He only saw a few workers running up to the mountain and running back down to the valley gathering for themselves and for the edification of the church, the gifts and the blessings that God has for all saints.

As Elias was in this valley, a mighty angel appeared at the top of the mountain. When the feet of this angel landed upon the mountain, blue sparks went everywhere and illuminated the land and the sky. His appearance was engulfed in such brightness, light, and glory that nothing on this earth can describe it. Indeed, the brightness, light, and glory that engulfed that angel spread forth from the mountain down to the valley. Before Elias, stood the most beautiful creature that he had ever seen. Words cannot truly describe such creatures as angels.

The angel said to him audibly though Elias was far away from him, "Come!" Elias got up from where he was sitting and began to walk toward the angel. The angel said, "No!" The angel pointed his finger and Elias began and continued to float toward him. Finally, Elias reached the angel who by his power set him down. At that point the angel said, "All those people who were shown to be doing nothing for the sake of Christ have been sitting right in the place where they were saved. They have not moved an inch. If these people are not extremely careful, they will be sitting right there when Jesus comes! All the gifts and blessings for my people are found up here upon this mountain if they will come!" The profound statement from the angel speaking in the person and voice of God still echoes within our minds as Elias expounded his experience from the Lord. We have never forgotten them! It has pushed us to do something and at least to meet God half way.

Lastly, before this translation ended, the angel showed Elias that Ricky was upon the mountain where the gifts and blessings are, receiving a hedge of protection over him. The prophet, Elias, and I had all prayed a week before this experience that God would do just that.

Symbolically, the mountain is Heaven. The valley is the earth. The few coming up and down are those who through prayers and beseeching God have entered Heaven and received the gifts and blessings of the Lord, which are for all if they will ask.

The second and last notable experience during this time was when Elias was coming home from shopping. He drove down Broward Rd. as he often did. Nothing was out of the ordinary. As he was approaching our home, he stopped behind a car. Instead of going around that car, he sat waiting. Suddenly as he waited for the two cars in front of his vehicle, the Lord spoke audibly, "Look up!" He looked up and saw a car speeding at 65 miles per hour behind him. He had only enough time to say, "Jesus help me!" before his car was hit. As he said that, a blue mist entered his car and surrounded him. The mist was visible and tangible. When the wreck occurred, Elias got out of the vehicle and said, "Well Lord, it is yours if you want Satan to tear it up!" A police officer heard what he said and thought he was in shock. A friend, who happened to be present, said to the police officer, "He is all right. He is a praying man and believes that the Lord has preserved him through this." So, God did! The car was totaled. Elias was fine. However, he began to feel the effects of the accident as he was lying down to go to sleep. He told Ricky, "I might not be able to wake you up for school." But at that moment, the Lord spoke to him and said, "Child, I have taken you this far. I can take you the rest of the way!"

Ricky was fourteen years old when the prophecy was given by the prophet. I watched him for two more years getting on the school bus and Satan speaking awful things to me. This was especially true when the weather would be bad and the school bus would have to travel over the Matthews Bridge. Repeatedly, I would say to Satan when he was telling me that he would kill my son, "Ricky is in God's hands. Satan, you cannot touch him!" I pled often the blood of Christ upon him. Satan fears the power of the blood more than anything else.

Having received the promise I became bold in the Lord. I went everywhere telling everyone that God was going to heal my son. People looked at me strangely. They thought that I was crazy and even said, "Poor Dot." Worst of all, some even laughed at me. I was laughed at many times within the two years before the miracle. Even my family did not understand what was going on. One of my sisters called, after Ricky had graduated from college, crying and asking forgiveness. She could not understand with her finite mind what a marvelous and mighty miracle God had wrought within our family.

Too often we seek and beg God for miracles and then when they come to our families, we reject them or deny that they ever came at all. Only by the grace of God does God still perform miracles, even when families and people in the church continue to deny them. Thank God for His grace!

6

THE MIRACLE AND ITS AFTERMATH

Between 1975 and December of 1977, Elias and I continued to have Ricky tutored every Saturday, even during the summer. While we had received the promise, we did not stand idly by and do nothing. We kept holding on to that promise! As I said before, that was all that we had to hold onto. We received the promise and that was all. There were very few signs that God was working. Yet, He was working behind the scenes placing pieces of the puzzle together. He showed His true mastery and handiwork. He truly demonstrated that He is the Great Architect.

In December of 1977, the life of Ricky was totally changed instantaneously. Ricky, his father, and I went to a Full Gospel revival at another church. The preacher, Al Edenfield, sang and sang. As he was singing, he went back to where Ricky was sitting and said, "Young man, you have a learning disability! Can I pray for you?" Ricky said, "Yes!"

The preacher put his hand on the head of Ricky, snatched it back off and said, "The Lord has heard your cries as you lay awake at night saying, 'Why can't I learn like other children?' If your mother would stand on faith and have you put in the tenth-grade, God would fill in the foundation!" It was as if all at once these words so struck me that I became paralyzed all over. I could not think nor realize what God had just done. Words cannot describe the state in which I found myself. However, thank God, the preacher knew that I did not understand or fully realize what had happened to my son that very night and instant!   The preacher caught me as I was going out the door and said, "Little sister, you did not understand what happened to your son! The Lord said that He had healed your son! In three days, University Christian School will call you to take him out of that school. The reason is that the teachers cannot help him and are using him as a baby-sitter in that 'Special Education Class.'" It was quite true that they were using Ricky as a baby-sitter. I knew that this was true because Mrs. Dugger had told me this. However, I did not become highly excited over what the preacher had said. I guess I was in shock and walking in the midst of a cloud.

My head continued in that state until the school called me the third day. The elementary principal, Mrs. Sanders, called me that day. She said that I screamed out to her, "Mrs. Sanders, the Lord has healed my boy! Put him in the tenth-grade! I will be over there in a few minutes!" Although the school was thirty minutes away, it was almost as if I flew to that school. I even broke the speed limit. I ran in that school yelling out loudly, "God has healed my son!" Can anyone just imagine what Mrs. Sanders was thinking? She must have thought that I was crazy, lost it, or had a nervous breakdown over my son. She sent me to the head principal of the school, her husband. I went and told him the same thing. Of course, at first he did not believe that God had healed my son. He said, "Mrs. Roberts, you are going to destroy your son! Jumping seven grades is impossible for anyone! This school has done all that it can do!" Thank God he had a Bible verse on the wall. It read, "But Jesus beheld them, and said unto them, With men this is impossible; but with God all things are possible (Matthews 19:26)." I told him very kindly but with holy boldness, "Mr. Sanders, if you don't believe that my son fits in that verse, take it down because you are a hypocrite!" All at once, I knew that he wanted to send Ricky to Doctor Smith, a psychologist, and have him analyzed. I said, "There is no problem with this. I have had Ricky analyzed by so many psychologists and psychiatrists that another doesn't bother me." Mr. Sanders said, "I do not want you to spend any more money." I told him, "Call your doctor!" He made an appointment with Doctor Smith.

The very first thing I told the doctor was that God healed him. Dr. Smith said to me, "I do not believe in that junk!" The doctor had already been informed about Ricky and his learning disability. I strongly said to him, "I am a believer and God's work can be tested! I want you to test God's work, whatever the cost!"

A few days later, Mrs. Dugger and I went for the report on Ricky from the doctor. He said, "I don't know what to tell you people! Put this boy up in the tenth-grade by all means! He was doing algebra, trigonometry, and all other tenth-grade work that he had never had!"

Mr. and Mrs. Sanders did not want to place Ricky in the tenth-grade unless it was agreed that the remaining part of the school year Ricky would be placed in the tenth-grade on trial to see if he could really do tenth-grade work. Remember that before December of 1977 Ricky, at best, was on a third-grade level.

Between Christmas vacation and the beginning of the next semester, Ricky prepared himself to enter the tenth-grade on trial, keeping his "Special Education Class" as his homeroom. If Ricky had failed, all would have been lost! Yet if Ricky succeeded, all would be won! It was death or life for Ricky. It was time for God's work to be truly tested! His whole future hung in the balance!

Although God had miraculously worked upon Ricky, the teachers did not want a retarded student in their

83

classes, even on trial. They still could not conceive that God had healed my son. Therefore, the label of retardation still attached itself to Ricky.

This was a terrible problem for Ricky, but it was no problem for God. Several months before God healed Ricky God had moved a teacher, Mr. Hazlett, from Pennsylvania to be a history teacher. He agreed to have a retarded child in his class since he himself was the father of a retarded child. Elias and I saw the very inner workings of God in all of these things. Each Special Education teacher had a part in this miracle. Each one played a valuable role in God's workings.

After nine weeks on trial, Mr. Hazlett called me and said, "Can we talk?" He said, "The first Monday morning after the Christmas vacation Ricky came into my classroom. The other students, knowing that he was a retarded teenager, began to laugh and giggle at him. His face and eyes were downcast. He began to tremble terribly. I set him at the front of the classroom. He took out his notebook and began to write down everything I wrote on the blackboard. I went very slowly in explaining the lesson. That first week there was a test on the subject material. Guess what? Ricky made a hundred, and in six weeks, he was tutoring the other students who had called him the big fat moron."

During this trial, other teachers also decided to allow Ricky to be in their classrooms after Mr. Hazett said he would have him in his classroom. Nevertheless, every teacher had to hand in an evaluation of how Ricky was progressing with his studies. This was not his report card.

At the end of the first nine weeks, Mrs. Sanders called me just crying and said, "I think you need to read the reports of the teachers!" I drove over to the school forgetting for a time the speed limit. Mrs. Sanders with a smile on her face said, "I would like you to read this report!"

The report of Mr. Hazlett read, "Mrs. Sanders, concerning one Ricky Roberts whom I have in my class, his average is a ninety-six. He is a well-behaved young man. Do you have any more Special Education students like Ricky? Please, send them to my class!" In that half of a year, Ricky made the honor roll, and he diagramed sentences in that same year, which he never know how to do that before his healing.

I will never forget the day that Mrs. Sanders called me. She was all excited. She said, "All the time that Ricky was in the 'Special Education Class,' I never heard him laugh. I heard Ricky laugh for the first time!" To Mrs. Sanders, hearing Ricky laugh for the first time was like discovering a long lost continent.

Explaining the joy that my husband and I felt is impossible when we came home from work and found Ricky doing his homework. He was never as happy as when he turned sixteen, and Jesus healed him.

When that school year closed, I went to Mrs. Sanders and asked for their best English teacher to tutor Ricky over the summer. She said that she would trust Ricky with only one teacher, Mrs. Glidden. She had taught college and worked for a book company as their main editor. I said that this is the one that God wanted for Ricky. That summer, she tutored him. She taught Ricky five times. Four of these five times she taught four different levels of English to him: elementary, junior high school, high school, and two years of college. The fifth time she spent two straight hours testing him to see whether he knew it. She came through the living room with her hands in the air praising Jesus about what He had done for Ricky.

In the '78-'79 school year, Ricky entered the tenth-grade for credit. The teachers were judging and looking behind each other. They wanted to make sure that he was truly earning his grades.

The very first day Ricky was called into the principal's office and was told that he would have to have U.S. History for tenth-grade credit. The teacher, Miss Cover, who taught U.S. History was extremely hard. No one had ever made a grade higher than a C in her class. She was going back to college to be a lawyer. Ricky told the principal, "God has not healed me to run from anyone! Give her to me!"

One day Ricky came home from school and I heard him on the telephone calling Miss. Cover about his report card. He said, "Miss. Cover, I have averaged my grade behind you, and I have a 'B!'" Miss Cover said, "Ricky, you did make a 'B!'" But Ricky said, "You gave me a 'C' on my report card!" Mrs. Cover changed the report card the next day. Ricky kept on working until he made two "A's" in her class.

Finding Ricky on his knees early in the morning was still very common. He often prayed himself to sleep. Sometimes his legs would be asleep, and we would have to help him into bed. While God gave Ricky the ability to learn, God demanded that he study, and so he did relentlessly. It was as if he had an unquenchable thirst for knowledge and still does.

In the tenth-grade, he was nominated for National Honor Society. He passed the entire year with four "A's" and four "B's." Elias and I received that report card with such joy that cannot be explained. For so many years, Satan said this could not be, but God said that it was possible. I thank God we believed Him and not Satan!

That summer Ricky began to teach himself about computers. He would need this very badly later on as God walked our family through what He wanted for Ricky's life and our lives.

One night in the eleventh-grade, Ricky was initiated into the National Honor Society with a beautiful candlelight service. The teacher, Mrs. Bishop, who was the sponsor for the National Honor Society for University Christian School said that night, "Lord, I am thankful for my son, but no one could be as thankful as the parents of Ricky are!"

That year for the first time in his life, Ricky could hold his head up high and all could see the joy on his face. Satan had lied to Ricky for all those years, but God continued to speak the truth. His eleventh-grade Ricky averaged seven "A's" and one "B."

In the twelfth-grade, he was given "Business Law" as a subject. The teacher, Mrs. Richardson, had been a substitute teacher in "Special Education Class" a few years before God had healed Ricky. She asked Ricky whether she had ever taught him before at University Christian School. Ricky said, "Yes, you taught me in the 'Special Education Class!'" She remembered and became dumbfounded and literally went in shock for a while. She could do nothing but remember Ricky in that class struggling to pronounce the word "and." Now, he was taking "Business Law" pronouncing twelfth-grade words and defining them.

In his twelfth year, he also studied "Old English" as part of a literature class. I could not understand why God would want Ricky to take "Old English," but in God's sovereignty, I saw later its purpose. Most of the books that we have bought are written in very "Old English." I cannot understand them, but Ricky can!

In 1981, Ricky received the "International Youth in Achievement of the World" award. Only ten-thousand teenagers are inducted annually. In 1982, during his first year of college, he again received that award.

The night Ricky graduated from high school he received every award but two. When he went up to receive his first award the principal, who at this time was Mrs.

Glidden, told Ricky, "Just stay up here, Ricky, you will walk yourself to death!" He earned the highest-grade average ever achieved in "Business Law," and was "Class Honor Student" and "Best Student in Religion." Elias and I had prayed that Jesus would receive glory and honor, and so He did!

That night Ricky also received the "Outstanding Award." Mrs. Glidden asked the question while Ricky was up there, "Why is Ricky receiving the 'Outstanding Award?' I don't think that he will disapprove if I tell you that when he came to this school he came mentally retarded staying in our 'Special Education Class' for about five years. Ricky said, 'His faith in the Lord Jesus Christ had grown, and Jesus healed his learning disability!' It does appear that this is true since he jumped seven grades, and that is impossible without God stepping into the situation!" After the graduation ceremony people gathered around Ricky wanting to know what had happened. Praise the Lord! The Lord received the entire honor and glory that night because of His grace!

After the graduation ceremony, the Lord spoke to Ricky. The Lord said, "I have taken you from the tail and made you the head. Now, Ricky, I want you to go on a fast!" That was so hard on Elias and me because it was the time that we had our garden and we were harvesting all the fresh vegetables. At first, Elias and I did not know how long the fast would be, but after twenty-one days had passed, we became upset. We began to cry and pray that God would help him. Elias would push his plate of food away and cry out to God to allow him to do that fasting for Ricky. Ricky had to fast for forty days without anything to eat. He could only drink water. What was so amazing about this fast was that one day before the end of this fast, God told Ricky that since he was obedient he could eat anything immediately after the fast was over, and it would not hurt him in the least. Ricky told his father and me what God had said. Ricky wanted to eat a steak, French fries, a salad, bread, and drink tea. Elias and I knew that eating so much was not recommended after a long fast, but here again, we obeyed the voice of God and cooked Ricky all that he had asked.

When the fast was over, Ricky sat down and ate all that we had prepared for him. Remember that for forty days Ricky had not eaten anything, but he ate all that we had prepared for him, and he suffered no harm. This was another miracle in our lives! Again, we saw that "Obedience is better than sacrifice."

When Ricky began to go to college, he went to a Junior College here in Jacksonville. I told the counselor about God healing my son and what God had done. She said bitterly, "He will earn it here!" I rebuked her, and said, "He had better earn it! At that high school, I paid for his education, and it was not given to him in the least!" When he was tested, he was in the second year of college. He went until the middle of the second year to the Junior College.

Before he finished the Lord spoke to him and said, "Come out of that college because you have learned all that I want you to know there. Your mother is not going to like this, but I want you to study the Bible and the books that I tell you to buy."

What God wanted was truly a shock! I thought that God would give him a degree in Computer Science, but the Father had other plans for my son. I knew that Elias and I could not have raised him without the help of the Lord. Elias and I had given him to the Lord. I was not going to get between God and my son. That would have been dangerous. I said, "Go pray Ricky and see what books God wants you to buy." In about an hour, he came out with a list of books. I turned off dinner, and we went to a

Baptist bookstore. The manager had never heard of these books. He thought we were making fun of his faith. He asked us to leave and we left.

Again, we found ourselves praying and crying to God. I asked God, "Are we going into fanaticism?" Elias, Ricky, and I went to other bookstores. The managers also had never heard of these books. All the way to work I could do nothing but cry and pray to God again. The next day the Lord led me to call a church in Oklahoma. At first, I found no help, but God said to me, "Try again!" This time I got through and told the woman on the telephone the story about God healing my son. She gave me a name of a man whose professional name was "the Book Finder." I called him. Thank God he knew about all those books! He told Ricky that he would help him find the books. God helped us find all the books, but He ordered us to buy them. Later God opened other doors and means by which Ricky could find other books. Right before my eyes the prophecy given when Ricky was fourteen- years-old was being fulfilled.

During this time, I would come home from work and find Ricky having twenty or twenty-five books on the living room floor reading them. He could summarize every page well and remember what subject had been discussed on a certain page. It was common for Ricky to come into our bedroom about three or four in the morning, wake us up, and tell us what he had found out from his studies.

The Lord did not always make it easy on us to find the book that he would tell Ricky to buy. Once the Lord told him to buy a book and we tried everywhere but could not find it. Ricky began to cry and pray to God. He told the Lord, "Lord, my father and mother will buy the book. Yet, we cannot find it. Help us." The Lord said, "Ricky, tell your mother to quit fretting! Call the Library of Congress and have them reprint it!" The Library of Congress made a loose-leaf copy for us, but as soon as we received it, we began to cry out again to God. For if one page was lost, the book would be useless. The Lord sent Ricky to a particular bookbindery company here in Jacksonville where the workers bound it.

One night after about five years of studying the books that God told him to buy and praying between 12:00 a.m. and 12:15 a.m., Ricky cried out to the Lord, "Lord, I have a doctorate in your sights. However, man will never accept me." The Lord said, "Render therefore unto Caesar things which are Caesar's; and unto God the things that are God's." Ricky said, "Father, are You telling me that I can go to college?" The Lord said, "Yes!" It was not long until the Lord showed him a college in North Carolina, Christian Bible College.

When Ricky started this college, the principal gave him a year of college free if he would do research for them. Ricky agreed. The officers of that college said that they did not teach Ricky. Ricky taught the college. Remember the prophecy!

Ricky spent nine years there. He received for the glory of God and the One who healed him several degrees: Doctorate in Theology, Doctorate in Greek, Doctorate in Hebrew, Doctorate in Aramaic, Doctorate in Latin, Ph.D. in Old Testament Studies, and Ph.D. in New Testament Studies. During those nine years he always made straight A's never making anything lower than an A minus. He graduated "Summa Cum Laude" and was the first student to graduate at Christian Bible College with a 4.00 G.P.A.

Though Ricky had nine years of college learning Biblical languages, theology, Biblical history, and Secular history, at the age of fourteen before God even healed him of his mental retardation, he was enrolled in the school of the Spirit, learning from the Holy Spirit about the spiritual gifts and how they must be used. From this age to the present, Ricky has been used greatly in the prophetic ministry, giving words of edification and comfort to the brokenhearted and in the gifts of healing and of working of miracles. Please, notice! Ricky in his state of retardation could not reach up to God, but God could reach down to him and even use the gifts through him.

Between 1975 and 2001, Ricky has had many supernatural experiences from the Lord. Beside hearing the audible voice of the Lord God two notable times, Ricky has visibly seen the wings of angels flying across his room. He has beheld the glory of God visibly in such intensity that it lit up his whole room and almost blinded him for a time. He has heard heavenly sounds that cannot be described or uttered by a human voice. He has smelled the sweet odors of heaven enter his room and the hellish odors of demons entering our home and his room. He has beheld countless visions that include the Lord God, angels, the demonic, and other such things. In visions, my son has seen heaven, the very throne room of God and even hell.

Of the many visions, which my son has seen, I will recount them in another book that Ricky and I are writing. In particular, I will recount my son fasting twenty-two days, and the very presence of hell entering his room for eight of those twenty-two days. I will never forget it!

Between 1982 and 2001, Ricky received other awards, "The Community Leaders of America" (1983), "Young Personalities of the South" (1983), "Young Personalities of America" (1983), "The Biographical Roll of Honor" (1984), "The International Book of Honor" (1985), "Who's Who in America" (1998), and "Who's Who in the World" (2000-2001).

The "International Book of Honor" award is such an award that no word can describe it. Ricky's name is found in a book where many well-known names have never made it. Many political leaders are not found in it. Yet, my son, by the grace of God, is found there. The "Who's Who in the World" award only inducts approximately 45,000 people out of the entire world annually. Yet again, there my son's name is found two years in a row. There again, only by the grace of God.

I have been asked so many times what I would have done with my son if God had not healed my son. That is a place I do not desire to go. I see nothing but grace over the miracle wrought for my son. That grace can come upon anyone if he or she will meet God half way. That is all that God ever requires.

However, I will say that when I do deliberate on that question, I have not regretted my boy one day. This would be true even if God had not healed him. We, both his father and I, were proud of him even before God healed him. We believed that God only gives the best gifts. It was Satan who damaged him. All suffering is a direct consequence of man's rebellion.

When anyone asks Ricky to describe this miracle of God healing his mind he says, "It is like living in a very dark tunnel for years. Then, suddenly, a match is lit. The small light from this match becomes brighter and brighter until finally the light engulfs the whole tunnel." All of this was done instantaneously. All of it was done by God internally working upon his brain. Not until Dr. Smith tested Ricky did we have any proof that God had done anything. Still, Elias, Ricky, and I held on!

Time and again Ricky has flashbacks about his sixteen years of retardation. A certain smell, image, taste, touch, or sound can bring all these memories back like a flood. God desires that Ricky never forget his state of retardation. For years there has been a recurring nightmare that Ricky has suffered. Ricky is sitting in a high school classroom not being able to read a word or failing a very important test and not graduating. Only when Ricky wakes up, does he realize that it was only a dream. Only in the last three years has this nightmare disappeared. It only disappeared when Ricky took authority over it. This dream did not come from God but from Satan. Satan was tormenting my son. Thank God the saints have the victory and power over Satan through the blood of Christ!

TESTIMONIES AND PROOFS OF A MIRACLE

A Statement from a Thankful Mother
by Dorothy Roberts

As already seen, I have written this work as a country mother who loved her family. I had no such thing as an ex-traordinary faith but only a simple and uneducated faith. I was simple in faith and in theology. I only knew enough to believe what I read in the Bible. No preacher, teacher, theologian, or any other scholar could take the words of life from my hands and from my life when it came down to my son.

I can say neither that I knew anything about prayer nor how to pray, except ending it in the name of Jesus. All I learned about prayer came from no other one but the Holy Spirit. It was He who led me all the way, and it was He upon whom I rested my faith and my case.

The parts of this book written by me contain my thoughts in my own style. It was not intended for them to be written in the style of a Ph.D. Instead, the style is simple, straight forth, and that of a country mother. I pray that this style will touch the heart of those in a state of hopelessness.

I encourage all seekers of truth and all who are in a hopeless state to reach out to God for the answer, to step out into the deep waters of our faith, to lay down tradition, and to listen to God rather than man. What God did for my family, He is well able to do for all!

A Statement from a Pastor
By Jeana Tomlinson, Co-Pastor of
New Covenant Ministries of Jax.

When I first met Dot Roberts, she did not know who I was. She was testifying to my son about the good things God had done for her own son, Ricky. Tears streamed down her face as she recalled all the years she interceded that God would somehow give her a miracle and heal her boy. I was so captivated by her sincerity that I listened intently for the duration of her testimony. I stood spellbound by her account of the three years of desperate weeping, which preceded one of the greatest miracles I have ever heard. Then, I assured her that I indeed felt that God had brought us together when I was formally introduced to her. She spoke as a modern day Hannah that wept centuries ago for a son that she could give back to God. In her desperation, God came through and granted her the desire of her heart.

My desire is that you will be as blessed as I am for the mighty deeds done in the mind and heart of Dr. Ricky. You will be particularly impressed at the significant role his mother, Dot, has placed in the final orchestration of one of the most spectacular signs and wonders of our day.

Does God still heal? Yes!

Will He do it for you? Absolutely!

Read and study this account and permit the God of the miraculous to move in your life. Learn from Dot's walk through tears how to summon the Sovereign. *Jesus Christ the same yesterday, and today, and forever.* (Hebrews 13:8).

Memories of a Teacher
by Sally Young

I first met Ricky at University Christian School in Jacksonville, Florida, in 1973. I was the Special Education teacher there and taught both the mentally handicapped as well as those who were significantly behind in their academics. At the time, Ricky was coming to our school from a regular sixth grade class in the public schools. I tested him, and he was only reading on a primer level, which is well below first grade.

Ricky was very sweet natured, wanted to learn, and had a desire to serve God. He loved the Lord. I remember one time I asked the students to give sacrificially to some missionaries, and we had a little box to put their offerings in. Everyone gave a little, but I remember Ricky gave all that he had. He was always that way. He was always loving, giving and caring. You could tell how much God was already working in his heart even at that young age.

I had Ricky in my class that year and the next. We labored every day on reading, language, and math skills. I knew I could help him, but I did not think he would ever catch up to his grade level. His mother would even bring him over to my house to be privately tutored in reading because she wanted to help him to learn to read and to become independent.

It was to be many years later that Ricky and his mother shared with me that he not only caught up to his peers but far exceeded them and myself in his education and college career. It was obvious that I had been part of a miracle of healing. Was I responsible? No, *God* had his hand on Ricky all along. In His plan, Ricky had to be far behind in his academics for God to work. If he had only been a year or two behind, people would not have recognized the miracle that God performed. In John 9:1-3, Jesus' disciples saw a man who had been blind from birth and asked Jesus who sinned that he had been born blind. Jesus answered "but this happened so that the work of God might be displayed in his life." That is exactly what God did in Ricky's life. God is being glorified through this not only in healing Ricky but by using him to teach and help others.

I am privileged to have taught Ricky and to have known the loving spirit of Jesus manifested in Ricky, but most of all, I glorify and praise Jesus for His mighty work. Our class Bible verse was Philippians 4:13,"I can do everything through him who gives me strength." Ricky proved that to be true! Praise the Lord!

Memories of a Neighbor
By Virginia Harrell

I was a neighbor of Elias, Dot, and Ricky Roberts. Ricky was born with severe learning disabilities. Ricky's private school kindergarten principal had recommended that he repeat kindergarten, but he went on to first grade, which he repeated. I had given Ricky's mother some word and math tutoring cards, but they did not seem to help very much.

In 1970, I was a substitute teacher in a public school third grade classroom in which Ricky was a student. When I asked the class to please stand and repeat the pledge of allegiance to our flag, everyone in the class stood, except Ricky. I had to say, "Ricky, you have to stand and say the pledge of allegiance." Finally, he stood up and went through the motions of the pledge of allegiance with the class. Evidently, his teachers had not pushed him to take part in class exercises, math, or reading.

Shortly afterward, I told his mother that she really should send him to the University Christian School's Special Education Class.

Years later when Ricky was 16, he came to my house to read for me out of a sixth grade reading book. I did not think he would be able to read very much of the page, but I was amazed to hear him read the words and to attack the really difficult words in the proper manner. This was truly a miracle. I remember this vividly because I did not think he would ever be able to accomplish even this small feat.

Memories of Mrs. Bruce Dugger

I taught a multiage special education class at University Christian School in the school of 77-78. One of my students, Ricky Roberts, was a sixteen year-old boy reading on a third grade level at that time. Most of the students had been in this class together for several years. They were like a family to one another in the midst of a world that was unkind to them. Ricky was very happy to spend a good part of his days helping the younger children learn.

I felt a heavy responsibility to teach and push Ricky to climb to higher levels. I began trying to push his reading, math, and language forward. Before Christmas, I agreed with others to have him professionally tested to see what potential he could actually achieve.

His mom, Ricky, and I visited Dr. Smith after the results were gathered to make an academic plan. Dr. Smith encouraged the school to let me put Ricky into some sophomore classes to see how he could cope. He was placed in World History and other subjects along with his Special Ed. class. I continued working with him on his reading, language, and math skills.

Ricky did very well, and the following year he was promoted out of Special Education and placed in sophomore classes this time for credit. A lot of hard work and great perseverance found Ricky graduating with honors a few years later.

Yet I must admit, it was not Ricky alone that accomplished all of this. Ricky, as he was, could not have been able to achieve any or all of this. I beheld the visible and inner workings of God first hand! I never will forget it as long as I will live.

Memories Of A Principal
By Margaret J. Glidden

Ricky Roberts (of Jacksonville, Florida) graduated from University Christian School after attending here for eight years. This young man came to University Christian School as a non-reader with learning disabilities of a severe nature. When he entered the school, he was placed in the Special Education Class since he was several grades below the classmates of his age. Although he was 12 years old and in the 6th grade, he was reading below kindergarten level. Ricky continued to work in a small ungraded class under the direction of a Special Education teacher for about 5 years. Things appeared hopeless to Ricky. But his trust in God grew. He could not visualize graduation ahead for him; the thought of having a diploma for himself was remote. He was about resigned to moving along without the success that others always appeared to get. He said, "I cried to God to learn, and He taught me!"

In the winter of 1977, something out of the ordinary happened to Ricky. In December, God (at church) moved upon Ricky by His supernatural power through a preacher laying hands upon him and completely and instantaneously healed him of all the learning disabilities that he had. Instantaneously, God filled in seven years of school (from the 3rd grade to the 10th grade). The slow improvement was not due to anything that man did, but God slowly improving Ricky's mental capacities so that at the age of 16 God could completely and utterly finish what He had started. If God had filled all the levels at one time, Ricky's brain would not have been able to sustain it.

Memories of Robin Schottleutner

In 1974, my husband and I took our first teaching jobs at University Christian School. I was to fill the vacancy left by the previous Special Education teacher, Sally Young. I believe she had developed the program from its beginning, and since I was inexperienced, I simply tried to pick up and continue where she left off.

When I think back on that classroom of children, ages ranging from six years to sixteen years of age, I remember Ricky as a big boy sitting at his desk doing seat work with all the concentration and effort that he could muster. Though our classroom was air conditioned, he would perspire as if the calculations of his math problems were a mile run. Scholastically, he was behind his age. The reading and math problems took him long periods of time to complete.

At various times, there were students Ricky's age who showed anger or embarrassment at being in the Special Education Class.

As he progressed in school, I'm sure many noticed the growing confidence he possessed. One of the last phone conversations I had with him before we moved away, showed me of his widening interests and his ability to give advice. He asked me if I had a garden, and I told him I was enjoying growing flowers. "Well," he said, "you ought to have a vegetable garden because you can eat the vegetables, but you can't eat your flowers." Though I continue to spend my time with flowers in the yard, Ricky's words still ring true.

There have been many occasions where my husband and I have spoken of Ricky's desire and determination to succeed in school. It brought us great joy to hear of his uncommon achievements and to know he has given the glory to God. Mrs. Roberts once asked me if I believed God could still heal. As I look back on her question, I realize she knew the answer to Ricky's needs rested in God's power and ability, not in the efforts of a teacher nor in her son's desire to learn.

Special Education, Year of 73-74

Special Education, Year of 73-74

Mrs Robin Schottleutner

Special Education, Year of 74.

Mrs Robin Schottleutner

Special Education, Year of 75.

Mrs Robin Schottleutner

Special Education, Year of 76

Mrs. Dugger

Special Education, Year of 77-78

March 27, 2000

To whom it may concern,

We knew Dr. Ricky Roberts as a retarded teenager, were present the night God healed him and saw personally the after effects of such a healing.

Sincerely,

Maggie Ann Cooper and daughter
Ruth D. Quenberg

From the back of the first report card in Special Education. This indicates that Ricky Roberts was reading below kindergarten level, yet being 12 years old.

Reading Level

[Sig..... - Pre-primer Level Book 2

113

For more information concerning Dr. Roberts, his mother, their schedule of events, their ministry, and donations to that ministry, please contact:

True Light Ministries
P.O. Box 28538
Jacksonville, Fl. 32218
A Non-Profit and Tax-Exempt Organization
Fax: 904-751-0304

For I shall bring forth truth out of darkness for the sake of my people.